MEMOIR OF A BANK ROBBER

Memoir OF A BANK ROBBER

Gerald Heckathorn

I dedicate this book to my father, who stuck with me through good and bad and worse, and to my sister Laurie, who started the process of turning my life around by bringing me to Jesus.

Overheard at a Poker Game in Madison, Wisconsin

Q: "Gerald, what was the biggest haul you ever had?"
A: "From one bank, or in one day?"

18 U.S. Code § 2113 - Bank robbery and incidental crimes

(a)

Whoever, by force and violence, or by intimidation, takes, or attempts to take, from the person or presence of another, or obtains or attempts to obtain by extortion any property or money or any other thing of value belonging to, or in the care, custody, control, management, or possession of, any bank, credit union, or any savings and loan association; or

Whoever enters or attempts to enter any bank, credit union, or any savings and loan association, or any building used in whole or in part as a bank, credit union, or as a savings and loan association, with intent to commit in such bank, credit union, or in such savings and loan association, or building, or part thereof, so used, any felony affecting such bank, credit union, or such savings and loan association and in violation of any statute of the United States, or any larceny—

Shall be fined under this title or imprisoned not more than twenty years, or both.

(b)

Whoever takes and carries away, with intent to steal or purloin, any property or money or any other thing of value exceeding $1,000 belonging to, or in the care, custody, control, management, or possession of any bank, credit union, or any savings and loan association, shall be fined under this title or imprisoned not more than ten years, or both; or

Whoever takes and carries away, with intent to steal or purloin, any property or money or any other thing of value not exceeding $1,000 belonging to, or in the care, custody, control, management, or possession of any bank, credit union, or any savings and loan association, shall be fined under this title or imprisoned not more than one year, or both.

(c)

Whoever receives, possesses, conceals, stores, barters, sells, or disposes of, any property or money or other thing of value which has been taken or stolen from a bank, credit union, or savings and loan association in violation of subsection (b), knowing the same to be property which has been stolen shall be subject to the punishment provided in subsection (b) for the taker.

(d)

Whoever, in committing, or in attempting to commit, any offense defined in subsections (a) and (b) of this section, assaults any person, or puts in jeopardy the life of any person by the use of a dangerous weapon or device, shall be fined under this title or imprisoned not more than twenty-five years, or both.

(e)

Whoever, in committing any offense defined in this section, or in avoiding or attempting to avoid apprehension for the commission of such offense, or in freeing himself or attempting to free himself from arrest or confinement for such offense, kills any person, or forces any person to accompany him without the consent of such person, shall be imprisoned not less than ten years, or if death results shall be punished by death or life imprisonment.

TABLE OF CONTENTS

ACKNOWLEDGMENTS

I'd like to thank everybody who ever listened to my stories and said, "You should write a book, Gerald."

I met the author of a book about the Wisconsin serial killer Ed Gein at a poker tournament, and I showed him my first attempt at writing about inmates I'd met in the hole at Waupun. He took it home for two weeks, and then he told me I should write about my own personal experiences in prison rather than about the other inmates.

That, in part, is what I'm doing here.

I entertained a lot of other poker players with some of my escapades, and they encouraged me to write my whole life story.

I contacted some publishers, but I didn't know how to write a book or how to submit a manuscript, and they weren't very encouraging. They told me it had to be written a certain way, with so many pages, and a bunch of other criteria. Even if I met all these requirements, one publisher told me: "Right now on my desk I have about a three-foot stack of manuscripts that I'll probably never read, and yours will go right on the bottom."

So I gave up for a while.

A couple years later, I contacted another publisher, who said I had to submit my manuscript electronically. Up to this point, everything that I'd written I'd typed up on a typewriter. I wasn't computer savvy, and the prospect of retyping the whole manuscript electronically was too overwhelming for me.

Then I started asking around the poker community in Madison if they knew anyone who could help me, and Matt Rothschild answered the call. He took really good dictation, asked some probing questions, and gave me a structure for this book. It's no exaggeration to say you wouldn't be reading this book if it weren't for him.

I'd like to thank the librarians at Madison Pinney Library, who graciously gave us a room for working on this book every Tuesday morning for 12 weeks. I hope I didn't disturb anyone with my colorful language.

Most of all, I'd like to thank my two lovely sisters, Laurie and Shelly, and their families for their ongoing support all these years. I couldn't have made it without them.

PREFACE

Yeah, I robbed a bunch of banks when I was in my forties, and I paid the price. So don't be an idiot and do what I did. Prison is horrific and traumatic! And robbing banks? It's not something you can do just one time and then stop. It's an addiction. You can be addicted to anything: porn, gambling, alcohol, drugs, and, yes, crime. If it'll give you a buzz, a rush, a thrill, or a high, it's addictive.

Like all addictions, robbing banks is really lonely and self-destructive. You end up lying all the time to everyone, including your loved ones, just to get what you need, which is another fix. Then you end up either in jail or dead.

Nobody should have to live like that. And don't kid yourself: Eventually, you're going to get caught. Everybody gets caught.

I spent the better part of 35 years – almost half my life! — behind bars, first for misdemeanor crimes and then I graduated to major felonies. It sure wasn't worth it.

What follows is my account of my life. You'll see the bad choices I made, and the consequences of those bad choices. A lot of what I'm going to tell you isn't pretty. I put bad karma out into the universe, and it boomeranged back. I recognize that, and I look back now with my guilt-filled mind, and I regret so much.

CHAPTER 1:

MY FIRST BANK

I got into some crazy stuff when I was young, and it was mostly drug-related, and I was behind bars for quite a while. When I finished up one of my prison sentences in California, I really wanted to do the right thing and turn my life around. I was living in L.A. at the time, so I looked through the ads in the papers and saw this big one for Bank of America: "Careers in Banking!" They listed various jobs they had available, from bank manager all the way to janitors. The one that caught my eye was for bank tellers. So I said to myself, "I can count money," and I called them up.

They told me to come on down and fill out an application, which I did. On the application, they asked if I'd ever been convicted of a felony, and I said no. They got back to me and told me we can't hire you right away, but you could go to our school, and they'd train me, certify me, and place me in one of their banks when I completed the course. There was a catch, in that it was going to cost me $1,500. So I scrounged around for the money, mostly by selling a some drugs for a couple weeks, I have to admit, and I went to the teller school run by Bank of America and Wells Fargo.

Three months later, I'd passed all the courses and got my certificate, and I was eagerly waiting to be placed.

But then the manager of the school called me in and said, "Sorry, we can't place you because you lied on your application. We ran a background check on you, and we found out you've got a criminal record. Ex-felons who've committed theft or financial crimes aren't allowed to work in banks."

I said, "You should have told me that before I started this."

"Well, you shouldn't have lied on your application," the manager said.

I was really pissed, so I said, "Give me money back then!"

"Sorry, we can't give you your money back," she told me.

I kept arguing back and forth with her like it was a game of tennis.

"You got to place me," I said. "That was part of the deal."

"No," she answered. "The deal was we'd place you if your background check cleared. I'm sorry. There's nothing else we can do."

Walking out the door, I just kept yelling, "I'll get my fucking money back. You'll see."

I felt so depleted and depressed after that incident that I reverted back to my criminal thinking and my criminal ways because when you have a criminal mind, you're always dreaming up crimes to commit.

I was living with my dad in a trailer park at the corner of Cerise and Rosecrans in L.A. He was going through hard times, and so was I.

One day, I was looking through the yellow pages under "B" for banks. I needed money, and I knew that's where the money was. And because of the course I'd just taken, I knew what the tellers were trained to do in the event of a robbery. They were supposed to give the guy the money, and be polite, and do whatever he tells you, and try to remember what he looks like – any scars, tattoos, or other distinguishing marks.

Before I started out, I wanted to know what the penalties would be if I got caught robbing a bank. So I went to the public library, and I told the librarian there that I was doing a research paper on banks and asked her to give me the statutes that covered banking. I'm not sure she believed me, but she directed me to U.S. Title 18 of the criminal code. I read that if I didn't use a weapon in the robbery, the most they could give me was up to 20 years. If I did use a weapon, it could be a lot worse.

So I figured I wouldn't use a weapon.

I remembered from the movies that the bank robbers were always passing a note to the tellers. And I knew, from my training as a teller, that when they were asked to cash a check, they would always turn the check over to see if it was endorsed.

I didn't have a checking account, of course. I was a street criminal. So to get some checks, I put the word out that I'd pay a bounty of $20 for anyone who could grab me a book of personal checks from their robberies and $100 for anyone who could get me a payroll check. My street friends delivered. I even got a check protector that companies use to imprint their payroll checks on.

Once I got the checks, I was good to go.

I'd take someone's personal check and fill out the front for cash, and on the back, in big bold capital letters, I'd type out:

"GIVE ME ALL OF THE CASH IN YOUR DRAWER. DON'T ALERT ANYONE OR PRESS ANY ALARM BUTTONS. DON'T GIVE ME THE DYE PACK. I DON'T WANT TO HURT ANYONE!!!!"

A dye pack, I knew from my schooling, breaks open and splashes indelible ink, with force, all over the money. It seeps through your clothing and deep into your skin like a tattoo that won't go away for weeks and weeks. So I wanted to make sure they didn't try that on me.

I was really nervous when I got ready to rob my first bank. I put on a nice suit and tie. And to cover my fingerprints, I put superglue on each one so I wouldn't leave any of my prints behind, and I headed out the door.

It was about 10:30 or 11:00 in the morning on a sunny, warm summer day. I picked the Bank of America in down-town L.A. Because this was one of the banks that Patty Hearst had robbed, they had recently installed bullet-proof plexiglass windows in front of the tellers, with a little slot at the bottom for customers to slide their deposits or withdrawals through.

I'm standing in line, with two people in front of me. It felt like an eternity. There's a guard standing right at the door. Soon, I hear a voice call out, "Next!" I walk over to the teller. I'm so scared and so nervous and sweating profusely. I walk up to the teller, and I slide her the check.

"Hi, how are you doing?" she asks.

And then, when she flips the check over to see if it's been endorsed, she sees the notes and starts heaving.

"It's OK, just do what it says," I tell her.

I'm frozen for a second as I wait for her to hand over the money. I've got big puddles of sweat under my hands, which I keep wiping off the marble counter. Finally, she places the money under the slot, and I grab it, but I'm frozen in fear, and I can hardly walk. I'm in a trance, and I'm woozy. The adrenaline is rushing through me so fast. I have to walk past the guard, and I'm so scared. I go outside and I'm walking faster and faster and I run to my car and drive away, clutching the money.

It was only about $3,000. But I was really happy.

After I calmed down, I thought, "Fuck, that was so easy!"

It was such a rush: It was like bungee-jumping or parachuting out of an airplane.

CHAPTER 2:

MY SPREE

The first thing I did after I got home from Bank of America was to try to give $1,000 to my dad. I was living with him in his trailer in L.A. at the time. He'd taken the trailer off the wheels and put it there permanently in the trailer park. He'd just retired off the railroad, and he started going to garage sales looking for expensive China to resell. He collected rare coins, too, and would trade them. He also painted houses on the side, which helped him pay the rent and drink his beer and smoke his cigarettes.

It was him, his big black dog named Bela, and me in the trailer. There were two bedrooms and a couch, a two-seater. Pops slept in one bedroom, and Bela slept in the other bedroom. I got the couch.

"Why does the dog get a bed?" I asked him once.

"Because she would tear up that couch," he said.

Pops wasn't impressed when I put the $1,000 on the table for him. He just stared at it, and kept petting Bela, which was what he did when he was nervous or angry.

He finally pushed the money away. "I don't want anything to do with it," he said. "It's trouble. Where did you get it?"

"Just take it," I said. "There's nothing wrong with it."

"You probably got it from some drugs," Pops said, "or you stole it from someone."

He knew me so well.

I then told him I'd won it at the casino, but he still didn't believe me. And this added to the tensions between us that had been growing. He had a list of legitimate grievances. I was coming home late at night, messed up, and waking him up. I wouldn't work on painting jobs with him very often—only when I needed money for a fix. I had drugs all over the place and he was worried that Bela would consume some of them and die.

The next day, I was supposed to work with Pops at 6:00 in the morning. I'd gotten in at 4:00 a.m. and had no sleep. I was dopesick. I told Pops I need to get a fix before I can work. "No dice," he said. "You got to work first, and then I'll even take you to go get your shit." So we drove off to the job, with Bela in the front suit.

We start painting, but I'm no good. I'm throwing up, I've got diarrhea, and I'm sweating like crazy. I'm barely working. After about two hours, Pop says, "That's it. If you're that fucking sick, let's go get your shit!"

He didn't like the idea of driving into East L.A., a high-crime area, but he did it. I rolled down the window with a $20 bill, and this Mexican kid starts walking up to the car. All of a sudden, Bela starts barking real loud and drooling, trying to get at this kid. He backs away from the car, saying, "No, no, no." So I have to get out of the car to get the heroin.

As soon as Pops starts driving us home, I start to cook the stuff in the back seat.

Pops asks: "What's that smell? What are you doing back there?"

"I'm not doing nothing," I say. "Just keep driving."

I get the syringe ready, and I'm trying to find a vein, but he's driving too fast, so I tell him to slow down and then pull over.

Once he stops the car, I find the vein and start injecting the drugs. He turns around and sees what I'm doing. "What in the hell are you doing? Why couldn't you wait till you got home?"

Then he broke down right there in the car and started crying. He didn't say another word on the drive home. Five or ten minutes later, he throws my clothes at me, and says, "I want you to get the fuck out of my trailer right now. Get out!"

At this point, I was so messed up on heroin that I didn't care. I moved out, and when I sobered up, I started to plot my next robbery.

I knew I had to try it again. But I was worried that the police would find me, so I decided to be careful and to change my appearance. I asked around and found someone who knew a make-up artist who did work for the movies. He hooked me up with this kit filled with prosthetics and theatrical makeup. I'd put on mustaches and goatees or wigs. From then on, I always wore disguises when I would go rob a bank.

Finding a bank to rob was simple: I'd go to the yellow pages again, and I'd find banks that had ads with little maps on them. I'd look at these little maps, and I'd see that there's the 405 next to it or the Harbor Freeway, so I figured I could just get lost in traffic right after I robbed it. I was looking for any banks that were close to a freeway so I could high-tail it out of there. And I'd bring a canvas deposit bag with me with the note inside, so I looked like I was making a deposit for a company.

So I started doing banks next to the L.A. freeways. I robbed banks in downtown L.A and the vicinity: San Bernadino, Forest Hills, Laguna Hills, Torrance, Gardena, and Riverside. I did them all the same way: With that note on the back side of the check. No problem!

I took some of the money and bought a nice black El Dorado Cadillac with cruise control from a dealership on La Brea Avenue. The guy didn't want to sell it to me because I was paying in cash, but he finally agreed.

For a couple of the banks, I used a driver. He was a big Black guy, and when he saw how easily I was able to do it, he wanted to do one for himself. So I was the driver for this one, which was in San Bernadino. I drive up, he goes in, and then I see him run out of the bank with this old man chasing him. I jump out of the car and knock the guy over, and then we just split. I found out later the old guy had a heart attack and barely survived.

I had to let my driver go after that. He wasn't a great bank robber or a dependable driver. He drank all day -- gin and juice.

After I burned out L.A. and Orange County and Riverside, I robbed banks in San Diego and Palm Springs. And I did rob some banks in Palo Alto and Oakland, too.

But after a while, I thought I better get out of California before the cops caught up with me. So I took my act on the road, moving east: Grants, New Mexico, Albuquerque, Phoenix, and so on.

It was always the same routine. I'd get a hotel room. As usual, I'd look in the yellow pages, yep, under "B" for banks. I'd get out a map to see which banks were near the interstate or near the state line. And I'd try to line up three or four banks in the same town to do all in one day, one after another.

Malls were good places for me because there'd be a bank in one corner of the parking lot, and another bank at another corner, and there'd be two other banks across the street. I'd knock off the first bank, and I'd head off to the second one, while the cops were going to the first one. And when they were called to the second bank, I'd be on to the third one. The cops were always playing catch up.

I changed my approach slightly after one robbery. As usual, I'd put the money in the canvas bag next to me in the Cadillac when, all of a sudden, I heard a small explosion in the bag. There was a dye pack in the stack of bills, and it was electronically set off. It shot red ink all over the money, and some of it seeped into the leather seat and left a permanent purple hue on the passenger side. So from then on, whenever a teller would hand me a stack of bills, I'd bend the stack to make sure there was no dye pack in it. If it wouldn't bend, I was prepared to toss the whole thing back at the teller because I'd know there was a dye pack in it.

I worked my way across the country. One time, after I robbed a bank in eastern Wyoming, I was driving down the highway as I got into South Dakota, and I saw a wooden sign that said "Casino, next exit." It took me down into a pretty valley, and about 10 miles later I came upon this little casino. It was a one-story-long building, and it wasn't much bigger than a gas station.

They were running a two-table tournament, and I was dressed in my fancy suit. Someone asked me where I got all my money.

"I rob banks," I said, and everyone at the table laughed. Then one guy said, "Me, too," and we all laughed again. I know at least one of us was telling the truth.

I got better and better at this. But it was always the same thing: I'd hand the teller that note, with the instructions on the back, and I'd get the money and split. I only took money from one teller per bank, which usually brought in $3,000 or $4,000. I didn't want to demand money from the next teller: too risky. I was all about in-and-out in a hurry, and on to the next bank.

I did this for about a year and a half. I worked five days a week, sometimes six, because some banks were open Saturday mornings in the malls.

I robbed banks from California to Maine and as far south as Georgia. But after a while, the buzz wore off, and it was no big whoop. It was just like going to work every day. I'd get up, I'd put my suit on, I'd get my note ready, and then I'd head off to the job. It got to be routine, and I was getting bored. In the middle of my spree, I got really confident. I'd say to myself, "How much money of MINE are you holding there?" as I pointed to a bank in the yellow pages I was targeting. And when I'd head off in the morning, I'd say, "I'm going to get MY money."

But then later on, I got paranoid, thinking that law enforcement was chasing me, which, it turns out, they were. I wanted to quit, but I didn't know how else to make money. I didn't want to go back to selling drugs.

Too scared to quit, I had to keep going, so started to live it up. In the big cities, I'd stay in the fanciest hotels, sometimes $1,200 a night. I'd call ahead, make a reservation for George O. When I'd arrive, I'd go to the check-in counter and say, "You got a room for George O?" And they'd say, "Yeah, we have your reservation." I'd ask, "Look, you take cash?" And I'd just count out the hundreds. Then I'd go up to the room and put my bags down.

First thing I'd want to do is to get high. So I'd shoot up some heroin and check my stash. If I was low, I'd leave the room, drive to the airport, buy a round-trip ticket to L.A., call my connection up, tell him to meet me at a motel across the street from LAX. He'd give me the room number, and I'd grab a cab and go to the motel and get the heroin, which was wrapped up in a plastic bag, which I'd stick in the crack of my ass, and I'd go straight back to the airport and take the next flight back to wherever I was staying.

If my stash wasn't low, I'd just go down to the hotel bar. Usually, there weren't a lot of people there. I'd be having a drink and I'd offer someone else a drink. If it was a woman, I'd say, "I'm not hitting on you, I just need someone to talk to." And if it was a guy, I'd just strike up a conversation. But within a few minutes they'd catch on that I was lying about something, or they'd sense that something wasn't just right with me, and they'd leave.

There was this one guy I was talking with at the bar for about an hour. But then he says, "I got to get up in the morning and go to work." I was so starved for conversation and friendship that I put $300 down on the bar and said, "Can you just stay and talk to me for another hour? I'd really appreciate it."

He says, "I'll sit here and have one more drink, but you don't need to pay me."

I was willing to pay people to be my friend!

But I couldn't trust anyone. That's what it's like to be a criminal. You're constantly on the move and constantly looking over your shoulder.

During my bank-robbing spree, I never got stopped by an armed guard in any bank, and I never got pulled over by the cops while I was driving away, or while I was moving cross country.

But I did have a few close calls.

Early on, I walked into a Bank of America in San Diego. It said, "Bank of America: Asian Branch."

There was nothing but Asian people everywhere. All the employees were Asian, and all the customers were Asians.

I go up to the teller and say, "High, I just want to cash this check."

She turns it over, sees my note, and hollers at me: "No,

you go!"

I didn't know what to do, so I grabbed the note and booked out of there.

Many months later, I was at a bank in Houston, Texas.

The teller was real talkative.

"Hi, how you doing?"

"Fine, you?" I said.

"You not from around here, are you?"

"No," I said, as I start handing her my check.

"No, I can't help you," she says. "Not if you're not from around here."

She hadn't even turned it over to see my robbery note.

I asked her again and urged her to turn it over and see that it was endorsed.

But she refused.

So all I could think of saying was, "Thank you, thank you," and I headed out.

Then I see that same teller in the parking lot with a piece of paper and a pencil. And I thought, "She's getting my license plates."

My third close call was at a bank in Chicago.

As always, I approached the teller and handed her my check.

She turned it over and saw the note, and she wasn't having any of it.

"Unh-uh, honey, I ain't giving you no money," she said. "You better get the hell out of here."

She was talking to me like I was a naughty little kid!

"Well, give me my check back then," I said.

She wouldn't do that.

So I grabbed one end of it, and she held the other, and we tugged at it, and it ripped in half.

She said, "I got half of it now, and you better get the hell on out of here."

And so I did, without further incident.

When I tally it all up, I figure I robbed somewhere around 250 banks and hauled in about $800,000, though the police said it was more like a million and three quarters.

CHAPTER 3:
MY CHILDHOOD

I was born in San Francisco General Hospital on April 4, 1950, to Jeannie Warren Heckathorn and Harold Heckathorn.

My dad worked on the Union-Pacific railroad, and mom was a secretary for a Chevrolet Cadillac dealership.

She liked to get all dressed up and go to piano bars at night and drink martinis. She had this infectious laugh and would sit around the piano and sing, though she didn't have a good voice. She'd be very loud and off-key, but she loved it.

Dad didn't like her going out all the time and getting all dolled up. He was tired after working 10 hours a day, and just wanted a good meal and to go to sleep.

They had different ideas about how to live their lives. They did nothing together.

My parents divorced when I was three, and she wanted my

older brother to live with her, and my dad wanted me to live with him. But my dad ended up getting both of us because Mom was a little irresponsible with her drinking. She didn't seem interested in caring for us. I didn't see her much at all after the divorce. Just a couple short visits once in a blue moon.

One day, my dad took me and my brother Don and put us in the back of his car and drove us to Beatrice, Nebraska, where his parents lived. And he basically just dropped us off. I was three and a half, and my brother was six.

The house my grandparents lived in was huge. They had a large yard, with a big old mulberry tree in the back. Grandpa even built a tree house in it for us. They had a beautiful spread, and it was only one block from the school we'd be going to: Stoddard Elementary School.

My grandparents were real strict. I don't think they really wanted us there. And if we ever did anything wrong, my grandmother would make us go cut a switch off of the willow tree on the side of the house, and then she'd whip us with it. We called it "getting switched."

One incident sticks in my mind: I was six, and it was the Fourth of July. Don and his friends thought it'd be fun for me to hold a lit firecracker. I did that, and it burnt the fuck out of my fingers. They were laughing their heads off, and my brother got me a Band-Aid for it, which didn't do anything. Then he had another idea.

"Hey Jerry, put this one in your teeth," he said.

So of course, I did, and it blew up in my face. It hurt like hell, and my grandparents rushed me to the doctor's office.

Back then in a small town like Beatrice, you didn't go to the emergency room. You just went to your doctor's office, and they'd see you right away. His name was Dr. Wildhaber. He fixed me up with a lot of cream for my burns, especially on my lips and the tip of my nose. I liked Dr. Wildhaber a lot.

When we got home, my grandmother told Don to go get a switch from the willow tree. We both got switched: Him for doing it, and me for being so stupid.

I was called stupid a lot when I was a kid. Here's another example. I was about seven or eight when my grandparents bought my brother a go-cart, and I was told never to touch it. One day, Don and his friends are out there, and they're taking turns driving the go-cart, and I'm watching, and I want to take a turn driving it. First, he says no, and eventually, after I keep nagging him, Don says, "OK , Jerry, get in. Take it up the road one time."

So I get in and drive up the gravel road and turn around. As I come back, I couldn't figure out how to stop the go-cart, so I panicked and I put both legs down to try to slow down, but the go-cart was still in gear, and the pulley just sliced my left leg right above the ankle all the way to the bone. You could look right in there and see the bone.

I was in excruciating pain, and I kept passing out. The kids helped me walk over to the front porch, and they set me up with my back against the screen door. Don yelled, "Grandma, Grandma." She comes to the door, but she can't open it because I'm leaning against it. So she starts yelling at me, "Jerry, move your ass away from the door." And I'm out of it. I don't know what's going on. Finally, Grandma managed to push the door open, and she saw how badly hurt I was. She told the other kids to get off the porch and go home, and she yelled for Grandpa to come, and they took me to the doctor's office.

Dr. Wildhaber told me I was going to need some stitches, so he got out a big needle to numb the skin so he could sew me up. But when I saw the needle go inside near the bone, I started to freak out and scream.

"You got to calm down," the doctor said.

My grandma said, "Gerald, if you stop crying, you can have this five-dollar bill."

Well, all I remember is that I had a death grip on that five, and I didn't let go.

Dr. Wildhaber sewed me up. I got about seven stitches on the inside and eight on the outside. And he sent me home on crutches.

Don, of course, had to go out and get a switch. He was the only one to get switched this time.

Every once in a while, whenever he was close by with Union-Pacific, my dad would come back for a couple days and take us out to McDonald's and have a lot of fun with us. But then he'd have to go back to work on the railroad, fixing tracks.

At Thanksgiving at my grandparents, all the family would gather, but Pops wasn't there because he had work. My aunts and uncles and cousins would come over, and the women would leave their coats and purses on the living room table. I'd crawl under the table and reach up and grab one purse at a time and rifle through it, grabbing a $10 or a $20. I got caught by my cousin Shirley, who was an elementary school teacher. She bends right down and looks at me and I have her purse on my lap and a $20 bill in my fingers.

"No, Gerald, you know better than this," she says. "I'm not going to tell your grandma if you promise you'll never do it again."

"I'll never do it again, Shirley, I promise," I say. "Just don't tell Grandma."

In elementary school, I met a kid named John Orwen. He lived across the playground from the school. His dad was in prison, and his older brother was a tough guy. We'd go over to John's garage, which we turned into our clubhouse. We were only eight years old, but we'd smoke cigarettes and drink beers and play music and talk shit and fight each other. Eventually, we'd go out and steal things from people's houses or shoplift from stores.

I was big and fat as a kid, and I'd throw my weight around, bullying the littler kids. I was the toughest kid in the fifth and sixth grades. Then a bigger kid came, and he started bullying me, and I figured that this bullying thing wasn't going to work in high school, which started then in seventh grade.

About this time, Don, who was a jock, started smoking weed and bringing girls home. And I discovered I liked drinking and getting high. My brother and his friends didn't want me hanging around with them, so I'd get my own beer and weed. The only kids who would accept me were the bad boys, and they egged me on, so I became a bad boy myself.

"Go steal that, Jerry," they'd tell me.

"I don't want to steal that."

"Stop being a pussy. You scared?"

And so I'd go steal little things from a gas station or a mom and pop store.

But if I'd had my head on straight, I'd have gone into my grandpa's business. He owned a plumbing shop with his brother: Heckathorn & Sons Plumbing and Heating. This could and should have been my legacy instead of the one I have now as a criminal. I should have been a plumber. Occasionally, he and my uncle would take me to work with them, which I enjoyed. And then, when I was in the ninth grade, we worked on the Alaskan pipeline together from Kansas to the Canadian border. I loved it. It was hard work.

But the lure of drugs, and the appeal of the hustle, got the better of me. I dropped out of school in the tenth grade, which didn't please my grandparents at all. I was up to no good and was acting up in a bad way.

One day, Pops bought a brand new car, a white Chevrolet Caprice. It was 1965, and I was 15. Two days after he bought it, I stole it. That night, I got shit-faced, and four of my buddies got in the car with me. I tried to take a curve way too fast and ended up in a ditch. My only injury was a broken thumb, so we got out and ran. I went home and went to bed. Next morning Pops called the cops and reported his car being stolen. I kept quiet.

The chief of police lived across the street from my grandparents, and his kids and me fought a lot so he really didn't care for me at all. He had me picked up and brought to his office.

He kept me in there for quite a while, grilling me. Eventually, he told me that the other guys already ratted me out, so he was charging me with stealing my dad's car.

Pops wanted to let the case go, but the chief had a hard-on for me, and he pushed it through. He charged me with joy-riding, a misdemeanor charge, and called me an "incorrigible youth." The judge sentenced me to reform school until I was 25.

CHAPTER 4:
REFORM SCHOOL IN KEARNEY

The Nebraska State Reform School had a huge campus, with buildings surrounding this big grassy area in the middle. But life there was pure hell. It was a lot like jail, with a bunch of kids trying to see who was the toughest kid there. I got beat up like everybody else, and the staff didn't do much about it. It was nothing short of extreme child abuse, in my opinion.

After about six months into my sentence, I decided that I was going to escape. Me and two other guys climbed the 16-foot chain-link fence and ran towards the nearest highway. Then I decided to split off from them, and I ran across some farmer's field, past a herd of cows, which was way scarier than I thought it would be, and the other two started hitchhiking together in jailhouse clothes. They were immediately picked up by the local cops, who had been alerted at once that we'd escaped.

I made it to a pay phone in a mall parking lot and called my dad, who was living in an apartment in Beatrice at that point. You got to know this about my Pops: He would do anything for me! He drove three hours, picked me up, got me a motel room for a week across the state line, and gave me $100.

Pops left me there, and I didn't call him for fear of exposing him for helping me in case the cops were listening in. Then I snuck back into town, at night, on foot and up the back stairs into Pop's apartment. It was late and everyone was asleep, so I jumped in the shower and put on some clean clothes. Pops gave me enough money for a bus ticket to San Francisco, and away I went.

About two days into the trip, the bus was pulled over and the Highway Patrol boarded it. They walked directly to me and did the whole, "Get on your knees, hands on your head," thing. They cuffed me and took me away.

When I asked how they knew I'd be on the bus, they said the ticket agent recognized my picture they showed around the bus station.

So back I went to the original jail.

While I was there, I told Pops to bring me some pot. Yeah, I was reckless, and boy, did I take advantage of my dad! I told him to get a big bottle of baby powder, empty it out, put the pot in the bottle, and then put the baby powder on top of it. He tried following my directions, but he didn't understand how to do it.

He got a bottle of baby powder and emptied it out. Then he put the pot in the bottle, but he didn't put it in a baggie. He just poured it in! And then he put the baby powder on top of it! So of course, I couldn't smoke it because the pot was now all mixed up with the baby powder. I was disappointed, for sure, but I thought it was funny how out of it my Pop was.

The judge sent me back to the reform school. Once there I was tossed into the hole, naked, with no blanket and with the air conditioning on full blast. I spent six months in there. That's what I meant when I said it was like being in hell. When I came out, they shaved my head and put me in the worst unit in the whole institution. I had to fight with strangers almost every day, and I was getting my ass kicked.

I got knocked smooth out, just dropped like a sack of potatoes, a couple times.

I got called in one day to go to the smoke room and get a hit. This big Black guy said, "You ain't 16, are you?"

"No, I'm 15."

Bam! And I woke up on the floor.

A couple months later, this white ex-boxer who worked in the clothing room called me and started asking me some dumb questions about something or other. It was just a pretext to get me out of eyesight so he could just smack me. I don't know why.

He dropped me in one punch, and I woke up in the clothing room to laughter.

That's how it was.

I did get one nice reprieve, though. It was getting on Christmas, and for a morale booster, the administrators had all of us draw cards out of a hat, and whoever won could go on Christmas furlough with a family for the holidays.

I happened to win the drawing, so this farmer comes and picks me up in his pickup truck and takes me to his beautiful farmhouse, which was on a lot of land.

When we pull up, he introduces me to his wife and his daughter, who happens to be sixteen years old and very pretty. At dinner, we're all sitting around the table, and she's sitting next to me. The farmer leads us in prayer, and she's holding my hand, which was getting me excited.

After dinner, the farmer says: "Why don't you kids put your coats on?" And he told his daughter to show me around.

When we get outside, she starts asking me questions: "What did you do to get locked up? How long were you locked up for? Do you have a girlfriend?"

Then she takes me to the stables. "This is my favorite one right here," she says, and when we walk in, she gives me a kiss, and reaches down and starts rubbing my dick.

Yep, we had sex right there in the stall, which smelled like wet hay and horse shit.

We go back in the house, and it's time to turn in. They'd given me a bedroom upstairs, and hers was down the hall, and the parents' bedroom was downstairs.

I can't go to sleep. I keep thinking about this girl. I'm wide awake around midnight when the door opens and she slides right in. We have sex again, and then she goes back to her room.

At breakfast the next morning, we all pray, and she's bumping my leg, and she's all smiles.

"You seem happy today," the dad says to her.

"Is everything all right with you, Gerald?" he asks me.

I'm looking guilty as can be, but I try to hide it.

"Yeah, everything's OK," I said. "I had trouble sleeping last night. It was a little cold."

"Sorry about that," he said. "We'll get you some more blankets tonight."

His daughter and I spent the next three days together. They had a sleigh, and her dad used the tractor to pull her and me and her mom around in it. And we went driving around in the truck, and she showed me where she went fishing.

At night, we'd sneak in some more sex. By now, I'm in love with this girl! I want to marry her.

But it's time to go back to reform school.

When we're leaving, her mom comes to give me a hug. She said, "We'll write you a letter from time to time. And you've got an open invitation to come back here."

Right before I get into the truck, I start to say goodbye to the girl, and she gives me a big kiss and shoves her tongue down my throat.

Her dad, who was just getting into the truck himself, said, "I hope you come back to visit us. Be sure to write us."

When he dropped me of at reform school, he shook my hand.

I told everyone at reform school that I'd fallen in love with this girl and that we had a lot of sex, but nobody believed me.

She wrote a couple times. And I wrote her back several times. I was writing love letters, and they were pretty explicit, and I had lots of x's and o's.

Then the letters stopped. Her dad must have read one of the letters I wrote. That was the end of that love affair.

Then disaster hit.

One day the administrators of the reform school took all us boys out on an outing to this man-made lake to go swimming. There was a dock that went out for like two blocks into this large body of water. And the boys we're running off the dock doing shallow dives.

They started daring me, "Do a swan dive, do a swan dive."

So, stupid me, I did that, and I crushed three vertebrae in my neck. It hurt so much!

All I could do was stand on my knees and barely say, "Elp!"

I walked on my knees all the way to shore.

When I got to the beach, I fell face forward, and screamed real loud: "Elp!"

Some of the guys come and step on my back. They're laughing and mocking me: "Jerry needs some elp."

The counselor, who was basically a guard, says, "What's going on over here?"

They repeat: "Jerry needs some elp."

"Heckathorn, get up."

I can't move.

"Get the fuck up."

"I can't. I hurt my neck."

He forces me up anyway, and takes me to the van, where he places me face down.

Two hours later, some of the guys come in and they're

hitting me and kicking me.

When we get back to the reform school, they help me get out.

"I hurt my neck," I tell the counselor again.

"You're going to have to go back to your quad and see the nurse in the morning."

I kept telling them, "I need a doctor, I need a doctor."

I was in horrible, horrible pain.

But the guys kept telling me to shut up.

The next morning, bright and early, I struggle to get up to the nurse's office. Her name is Sleep, Nurse Sleep.

If you had a problem, you saw Nurse Sleep.

I told her I hurt my neck.

She said, "You just need a massage."

She gets this analgesic balm, which smells medicinal, and she starts rubbing my neck.

"Hold still," she says.

I'm in pain.

Finally, she says, "You're just going to have stay here overnight."

Next morning, she comes in and says, "How you feeling? Any better?"

"No, I need a doctor."

She pulls out this analgesic balm and starts massaging me really light on my neck. The she starts massaging me further down my back. And she keeps going down and grabs both my ass cheeks and then grabs my dick, which is on fire now.

"What are you doing?"

"If you're going to complain, I can't help you."

So she walks out, and locks the door.

Next morning, a counselor comes in.

"What's going on, Gerald? The nurse says you're giving her a hard time."

"I need a doctor! My neck's hurt, and the all the nurse is doing is giving me weird massages."

"You're going to need more than that if you keep talking about the nurse like that. You're going to the hole."

He dragged my ass there and put me on the concrete floor.

Three days later, he pops the door and asks, "How you doing now?"

I'm lying on the concrete fall in my boxer shorts in the fetal position, and I've been crying my eyes out. "I need a doctor," I say. "I hurt my neck. I need 'elp."

He says, "Do you need elp, or do you need help?"

He's being an asshole.

I repeat the story about the diving accident.

He's like the fifth person I've told the story to now.

He just leaves me there, and I don't know whether he's going to help me or not.

I was in the hole for another three or four days. Finally, a couple guards came to my door, gave me my clothes, and told me to get dressed. I was in a lot of pain. It was hard as hell to get my shirt on over my head. They handcuffed and shackled me and walked me downstairs, broken neck and all. I could hardly walk I was in so much pain. Every time I took a step, I got a stabbing pain in my neck. We had to walk across the yard to where an ambulance was waiting at the administration building.

The medics took a look at me and asked me what was going on, and I told them the whole story all over again. They put a collar on me and put me on a gurney and said, "This guy's got to go to the hospital now. He's got a broken neck."

They take me to this emergency room all chained up like John Gotti.

The doctor examines me and tells the cop: "You're going to have to take the chains off."

The cop didn't like that, but the doctor insisted.

"He's not leaving here," the doctor says. "He's got a broken neck."

"They should have brought you in right away," the doctor tells me. "We're going to put you in traction."

They had pullies on the wall with 30-pound weights. I had headgear with a strap under my chin, like a strapped hard hat. And I couldn't move.

I laid in bed like that for two-and-a-half months, and then they put the cast on me all the way down my body to my midsection.

I couldn't bend over for another two and a half months, and it was difficult to piss. I could walk, but I was just top-heavy.

One of the hospital employees took pity on me. He asked me if I wanted to smoke a cigarette, which was strange since no one was allowed to smoke inside.

"Yes," I told him. "I'd love one."

So he strapped me to a two-wheeler and pushed me to the

elevator and took me outside. He was a smoker, too. We did that a half a dozen times before we got caught and he had to stop doing it.

As soon as I could walk, they took me back to reform school with the cast on. Even then the abuse didn't stop.

These twin Black guys were bullying the new kids and taking their commissary.

I thought, "What could they do to me? I'm in a cast."

But they hit me in the face a couple times, and then went back to stealing the kids' stuff.

When I got back to the quad, I'm standing in front of my locker in the bathroom The next thing I know I got whopped in the back with a baseball bat, which broke part of the cast. I fell to the floor and couldn't get back up. A Black friend of mine saw me go down, and he came in and pulled me up.

I went to the guard and told him I'd fallen down and broke my cast.

"Who did that to you?"

"Nobody did it," I said. "I just fell down."

"How many times did you fall down? Who did it to you?"

"Nobody. I just fell down," I repeated. I wasn't got rat anyone out, and he didn't pursue it further.

He gave me a pass to go see Nurse Sleep. She wrapped some white tape around my case and told me that she was going to call the doctor to fix the cast.

The next day, the van was waiting for me, and they shackled and handcuffed me and sent me to the doctor, who recast me.

Weeks later, I got the cast off. They cut the cast in half and then in sections. It felt great to be free of it! And then I got in the bathtub, and the water turned black. I hadn't bathed in six months.

My neck eventually healed in a half-assed way, and I was given a "hardship discharge" after my Pops started raising hell about the way I was treated. I think they were worried about a lawsuit, but I really don't know what happened. I was just happy to get out.

CHAPTER 5:

STATE PEN AT 17

I didn't really learn the right lessons at reform school. If I learned any lesson there at all, it was how to inflict pain and torture on another human being. Might have been my fault, might have been the school's fault. Probably a little of both. But instead of reforming me, it hardened me.

And because I had unrecognized and untreated mental issues, my rebelliousness was out of control. I was fat, aggressive, unathletic, hyper-active, unloved except by Pops, and discounted. After being told you're a piece of crap, you start trying to live up to that, and so I did.

After my release, I thought I was a tough guy, and I talked shit to everyone. I took drugs and booze from people at parties, and I dared anyone to have a problem with that.

I started breaking into more places and doing petty thefts.

I broke into this one grain elevator in the nearby town of Wymore. All they had in the cash drawer was change, and a bag of quarters underneath. So I took all the coins and went to the truck stop, which was a den of iniquity. It's where the hookers hung out, and you could get any drug you wanted. We were too young to hang out at the bars, but we'd hang out at the truck stop and party in the parking lot there.

At the truck stop, I'm getting hungry, so I go in, and I order some food, which I pay for with the stolen coins. I flirt with the waitress, and when she goes on break, we go out to her car for some fooling around. When her break is over, we both go back inside.

The police come by and start asking the staff whether any customer has been paying only in coins. The waitress says, "Yeah, Jerry's been paying in coins. He's over there at the pinball machine."

The cop asks me, "Where did you get all this change?"

Sticking to my practice of lying and denying, I reply: "I've been saving up."

He just grinned and said, "Gerald, we know you robbed this grain elevator in Wymore, so you might as well stop lying."

They took me to jail and charged me with breaking and entering, burglary, and petty theft. But they let me out on probation on the condition that I live with my grandparents and that I report to my probation officer once a week.

My grandparents weren't happy with me, as you can imagine, and I was told I needed to get a job if I wasn't going back to school, so I found a job as a bellhop at a local hotel.

I became friends with the woman who ran the front desk. One day I'm talking with her, and she asks me if I'd watch the front desk while she goes to the bathroom. As soon as she leaves, I open the cash drawer and swipe a $20 bill.

As soon as she returns, I blurt out, "Nobody came," and I quickly returned to my bellhop station near the elevator.

"Thank you, Gerald," she says.

After the hotel did their books, they found they were $20 short, and they suspected I'd taken it. So they decided to set me up a few days later by marking every bill in the cash drawer.

Unsuspecting, I come to work as usual, and at around lunchtime, she asks me to watch the front desk again while she goes to the bathroom. So I go behind the counter and pull the drawer out and snatch another $20.

After she comes back, I go to my usual spot by the elevator. Suddenly, the cops barge in, including the chief of police.

I'm escorted to a back room, handcuffed, and questioned.

"Gerald, did you take any money out of that drawer just now?" the chief asks.

And like a little kid who stole the candy bar and has chocolate all over his face and still denies it, I say to the chief, "No! I didn't take any money."

So then he pulls out a black light and asks me, "Do you know what this is?"

"It looks like a miniature black light," I say.

"Put your hands out in front of you, Gerald."

"Why?"

"Just put your hands out. I want to show you something."

So I stick my hands out, and I see that they're covered with something.

"I must have got something on my hands," I say, and start rubbing my pants to get it off.

"Do you see that?" he asks. "That's ink. We marked every bill in that drawer. And we were watching. We saw you take the money.

Are you still going to deny it?"

"I don't know what you're talking about," I say.

Then he puts the black light on my pocket, and he can see the trail I left by sliding the money in.

"Gerald, look, we know you slid the money into your left pocket, because you've got ink on your pants," the chief says.

Then they tell me to turn my pockets inside out, and the $20 bill is in my pocket.

They take me to the county jail and charge me with second-offense petty theft, which makes it a felony.

There was this 65-year-old guy in the jail named Charlie. He was an ex-boxer, but he was still very muscular. We became friends, and just before I was to be released, he sent a message to his girlfriend, who was 30, to get some booze to me when I got out so I could bring it back to him, which I agreed to do.

My dad, who was in Beatrice at the time, shacking up with his girlfriend, bailed me out. Late that night, I drank some liquid courage and went to the outside of the jail with some weed and two fifths of Jack Daniels. But the bottles wouldn't fit between the bars, so I turned the bottles upside down and poured the liquor through the bars into the cups the inmates were holding. Then I broke the bottles into a bag and pushed that through the bars, too, so they could get rid of the evidence in the garbage. I didn't want to get caught outside the jail with empty whiskey bottles.

The sheriff lived upstairs with his wife and a German shepherd, and the dog started barking. The sheriff came down, and I took off running but I tripped, and he caught me.

So there goes Pop's bail money, and they put me back in the county jail. But I had a drink waiting for me – and a fatty.

I made a deal to get a year and a day in the State Penitentiary in Lincoln for second-offense petty theft. This wasn't reform school or Daddy Day Camp. This was the adult prison.

I was shaking as the bus drove up to the 60-foot walls and the gate opened. This was a real prison with men who would kill me if I said or did something they didn't like. I knew I needed to get it together and stop shaking before I got inside.

As I step off the bus, I heard guys screaming shit like, "He's mine," and "I'm going to fuck you!" The guards are just laughing, and I'm getting pissed. I decide to smack the first guy that gave me any shit at all.

The process for entering prison begins with an extremely thorough search and then a whole lot of personal questions. They asked me about my medical history, my family history, even my sexual history.

Then I had to strip down. They checked every piece of clothing, inch by inch. They told me to run my fingers through my hair, and then they had me flip both my ears to see if anything fell out. Then they told me to open my mouth and stick out my tongue and pull my lips up and down to see if I was hiding anything in there. Using a flashlight, they looked into my mouth and up my nose. Then I had to lift up my nut sack and dick. Next, I had to turn around and show the bottoms of my feet and wiggle my toes. Lastly, I was told to bend over and spread my butt cheeks and cough several times in case I was hiding something in my asshole.

After that, I had to hit the showers with 10 of my new-found friends.

So about smacking the first guy that gave me any shit, well, I discarded that notion and decided to just stay in the background and be quiet as long as possible.

After the shower, I was given my prison clothes, and we were ushered into a big dorm. That's where they give you all these tests to see what your capacities are so they can place you as far as work goes.

In the dorm, you're sleeping on double-decker metal bunks welded to the floor in this huge gymnasium. While you're in there, you're allowed commissary if you have money on your books. Not a lot of people had money on their books. But I had money, and once I ordered my first commissary, the vultures came out.

"Let me have some soap. Let me have some toothpaste. Let me have some deodorant," they'd say, and they'd promise to pay me back next week. They'd act all friendly when they're asking for this.

But I only had like $20, and I couldn't afford to buy them stuff, so I told them no.

Soon I'd hear three or four guys talking to each other: "We're going to get that fucker tonight," they said. "We'll just split all of his shit up." They said it loud enough for me to hear, and then they would look over at me.

I was scared to death. Just before bedtime, one of the guys came over, and said, "Look, you're either going to have to give up your shit, or it's going down tonight."

"What's going down tonight?"

He just laughed and walked away.

So I'm lying there in bed and I can't sleep. I keep thinking about what he'd said.

It's late at night. It's dark. People are snoring. Unbeknownst to me, these guys are moving like Ninjas toward my bed. They'd stuffed some tube socks with bars of soap and rocks and combination locks. As I'm lying there on the top bunk, I hear some rustling around me, so I sit up. Then this blanket comes over me and these guys are holding it down on top of me. And then they start to beat me with the loaded socks. They called it "Locks and Socks."

They beat me bad, and it hurt like hell. I had lumps and bruises all over my head and my arms and my body. When the lights came on the next morning, I was lying on the floor, and the guard finds me. I look like Quasimodo.

"What happened?"

"I don't know," I answer.

So he wrote it up that I must have had a bad dream and that I'd fallen out of the top bunk. Right!

But I didn't tell him I got beat up. I knew better than to

rat on anybody. I never ratted on anybody. I always rode my own beefs, which is what we called our own crimes. I took responsibility for them. I even rode other people's beefs.

I went to the infirmary for a couple days, which is just a cell with a hospital bed. And from the infirmary they put me in a four-man cell with a guitar-playing hippie, a wannabe tough guy white kid, and a pale white blue-eyed kid who looked like he was 13.

Right off the bat, we got along real good. We were all young and counter-culture. The hippie pulled out some pin joints that he'd smuggled in somehow, and we all got high on that very first day. We put our heads together to figure out how we could get more weed, and we encouraged visitors to bring us some. And I reached out to people I knew in the community to hook us up.

So it wasn't too long before we had enough weed to sell joints to other inmates.

One day these gangbangers from Omaha come up to our cell.

"We want all your weed."

"We only got 12 joints left," I say. "We'll give it to you for $20."

"No, you don't understand," one says. "Just gimme all your weed!"

"We're not going to give you anything," I respond. "If you want anything, you got to pay for it."

"You're going to give us the weed, or we're going to fuck each and every one of you up."

And they took off.

I'm freaking out.

The wannabe tough guy, Tad, is saying, "I ain't scared. I can handle those motherfuckers."

The pale little kid, though, is in tears.

I said, "We're not going to give shit away. But you gotta watch your back."

Tad says, "I'm going to go scout around." The rest of us are kind of panicked, including me.

Then the gangbangers show up again.

"How 'bout now? You going to give us the weed now?"

"Why now?"

"Because your boy: He ain't coming back."

"What happened?"

"He's in the hospital."

We found out later he was in intensive care. They fucked him up real bad. He had a concussion and lapsed into coma.

A guard came up and told us Tad wouldn't be returning, so we rolled up his personal belongings and handed them to the guard.

The next day, I go out of my cell for lunch, and as soon as I go down the stairs, these guys are just waiting for me. I look off to the left, and I see there's a guard standing there, just three feet away.

So I yell: "Officer, officer! I need to ask you a question right now."

"What do you want?" he asks.

"What happened to my cellie?"

"I don't know," he says, being a dick. "Put in a kite."

A kite's a form you write your question on. It's like a snail-mail message to the authorities.

"These guys are out to get me," I tell the guard.

He tells the gangbangers to get lost, and they slowly disburse.

I go back upstairs and get back in my cell.

I tell my cellies, "We can't leave our cells. It's not safe out there."

But the guitar guy had already put a kite in before all this to see the nurse. Later that day, a guard comes and gets him to take him over to the nurse.

First, he has to cross the yard to get there. It's about half a football field. You have to go right past the mess hall and the weight yard, which has a chain-linked fence that's 16-feet high. As the guard is walking him over there, he's cuffed up and gets about halfway from the cell house to the administration building when weights come flying over the fence like frisbees. The guards are ducking and running, as the disks are landing all around him. He luckily gets to the door of the administration building without getting hit, and the guards buzz the door open and he goes in.

"Just lock me up," he tells the guards and the nurse. "I'm scared shitless."

He never came back to the cell.

Next day, I asked the guard, "What happened to my cellie?"

"He PC'd up." He got in protective custody. He volunteered to go there.

So I told my other cellie, the kid: "You got to PC up, too, otherwise they're going to kill you or fuck you or both."

"OK, I'll go to dinner with you and then I'll PC up," he said.

"OK, good deal."

We go to dinner, and he was in a hurry to get back to the safety of the cell, but he got snatched up on the way back. They dragged him down underneath the boxing ring, and four lifers raped him over and over and then beat him and left him there bloody and broken.

The guards spent a whole day searching for him, and once they found him, he didn't know who did it. But we all knew who it was. You heard these guys laughing about it, and how he cried, and how he wanted his mommy.

We should never have been put in a prison like that. Not for the crimes we committed or how young we were.

Soon, the gangbangers came to my cell. Now I'm the only one left.

"Now you going to give us the fucking weed?"

"I ain't giving you shit. Fuck you!" I light up a joint and blow smoke in their face.

"We're going to get you, motherfucker! We're going to get you."

I didn't leave my cell for five days, and I got sympathetic inmates to bring me back some food from the chow hall. Meanwhile, I took a mop handle, and I wrapped black tape around the end of it, and I outfitted it with roofing nails poking out so it resembled a medieval mace.

I kept this improvised weapon above the little ledge next

to the door of my cell.

One day, one of the gangbangers comes back and says, "I can keep everyone off you if you just be nice to me."

"What do you mean?"

"Well, why don't you suck my dick?"

"I'm not sucking your fucking dick."

So he leaves, but he comes back often over the next few days with the same combination of sweet talk and threats.

I was sick of it, so I decide to do something about it.

The next time he came to my cell and told me to suck his dick, I said: "Put it in here through the food slot and I'll suck it if you promise you'll keep them off me."

So he pulled his dick out and laid it right on the platform, and I slowly reached up and came down quick and hard with my mop handle. I nailed him three times with it before he could move.

Blood was spurting out all over the place!

"You cut me, you motherfucker, you cut me," he screamed, and backed away from my cell, almost falling over the railing, 20 feet to the hard concrete fall, which would have killed him. He left, holding his crotch.

Later, the other gangbangers came for me.

They were huddling around my cell, screaming at me -- eight or ten deep.

Finally, a guard comes up and tells them to get out of here.

I told the guard: "You just gotta lock me up. They're trying to kill me."

"Who's trying to get you?"

"I can't tell you that," I said.

"Well, the only way for me to put you in the hole is for you to voluntarily put yourself in protective custody."

"I can't do that," I told him, because I'd look like a rat.

So I went back to my cell and talked to one of the guys who was bringing me food. He worked out at the automotive shop, and I asked him if he could bring me some gas. The next day, he brought me a little baggie of white gas when he brought me my food.

I took the gas and put it in a little plastic fruit cup that was empty and when they racked my doors in the morning for breakfast, I grabbed the cup and I walked as fast as I could to the gangbangers' cell and tossed the gas in there and lit with a bic lighter.

I went straight downstairs to the guard shack and said, "Is that enough for you to put me in the hole?"

"Just a minute, Gerald," he said. "Something's going on." And he went to check out the fire.

Finally, the sergeant comes back just as some gang members are coming after me.

"Break it up, guys," he said. "Break it up. We're locking it down. You, too, Heckathorn."

"Wait a minute, Sarg, I'm the one who torched that cell," I said. "You gotta lock me up for that."

So they put me in the hole, which was down in the basement. It's basically a long hallway with a dozen cells. There are bars on the front and heavy-duty screening on the bars. It's very dark and cold down there.

Still, the gangbangers were able to harass me while I was in there. They could see my cell if they hung someone upside down over the edge of the first tier. They made makeshift blowguns out of plastic straws, and for darts they'd use needles that they'd pissed on and then poked them through tiny pieces of cork. Then they'd shoot these darts through the little holes in the screen on the front of my cell. Most of them would miss me, but they hit me in the head a couple times. I got a huge knot on my head, which was infected, and I had to get treatment for it.

The next thing they did was to get into fake fights with each other so the guards would take both of them to the hole. They would do this over and over so they could fill the hole up with my enemies. The idea was that one of them would end up in my cell and could kill me.

The first guy who got put in my cell was gay. Right away, he told me what the plan was. He told me everything. But then he said: "I don't want to kill anybody."

We talked it over, in whispers, and here's what we decided to do. We'd pretend to fight so he wouldn't get beat down for not doing what they told him to do. We started hitting the walls with our fists, and he's yelling, "I'm going to fucking kill you."

All the other gangbangers heard us and were screaming: "Kill that motherfucker! Get him!"

The guards heard the commotion and came over.

"What's going on?"

"You better get this motherfucker out of here," I said, "or I'm going to kill him."

So they took the gay guy out, and I could hear that they

were getting ready to put another gangbanger in my cell. I grabbed my sharpened toothbrush, which was my home-made shank, and pressed my back against the wall as I waited for the door to pen. After the guards left, the new guy came at me. I put the shank up to his throat, and said, in a whisper, "I know what you're here for, motherfucker. Look, if you just be cool, you can make it out of here alive. There's no reason for you to hurt me, and no reason for me to hurt you."

For three days, we were in there together, and we were both scared. We could hear every sound and every movement, and neither of us got much sleep. But I was the only one with a weapon, and he knew that.

They let him go after those three days, and everybody else they put there in the cell with me didn't want to do anything. One reason for that was that I had canteen privileges in there because I'd been in there so long, and I had money in my account. So in my cell I had all kinds of food and candy and tobacco, which I shared with whoever came into my cell – actually as soon as they came in the door.

Eventually, the gangbangers gave up and left me down there by myself.

While I was in the hole, I was acting out and doing crazy shit. I'd be talking maniacally and crying hysterically and laughing at the same time, so they sent me to the state nuthouse to be evaluated for 30 days.

There were several buildings at the institution. The administration building was like an old limestone castle, and the other ones were old red brick. As you drive up to the place, you go through these brick pillars with a wrought-iron arc on top and a sign in the middle that says "Asylum." Then the road just goes in a half circle in front of all the buildings, and at the end of the half circle is another wrought-iron sign at the exit that also says "Asylum."

They brought me into the administration building, and they handed some paperwork to the guy at the door, and they took the chains off of me, and the psych tech escorted me to this big day room. Off of the day room were these three hallways where the bedrooms were. Every day, it was mandatory to stay in the day room with everybody else.

There was this Hell's Angel in there named Jimmy, who was really crazy. He'd walk around with no shirt on, but just a blue-jean vest with his club colors on the back and MC Rocker. Jimmy and me became good friends. I had long hair, and he had long hair. We talked about drugs and getting high all the time, and he loved talking about bikes.

After about a week there, one Sunday morning he says to me, "Come on, we're going to church."

I thought it was really weird, but we get in line with a lot of people, and the guard takes us through these tunnels. The whole way Jimmy is laughing and giggling and pointing to this door and then another door, saying, "You don't go into that one," he says. "But it's coming up."

We finally get close to the prison church.

"This is the money shot. This is the one. This is it," he says.

So we go up fives stairs to the church door and head on in. It's just a small chapel, and the minister is leading the service.

Jimmy's being really vague about why we're even at the church, and he's complaining throughout the service that he wants to leave. So I'm confused.

When the service is over, we head back with everyone.

On Monday, Jimmy says: "Next Sunday, you're going to be eating good: All the free soda and ice cream you want."

I still don't know what he's talking about.

Sunday comes.

"We're going to church," Jimmy says. "Grab all your shit. Don't leave anything behind. You won't be coming back."

"All right," I say, and I grab my toothbrush and my personal papers and stuff them in my pockets. The guard comes and tells us to line up. Jimmy tells me to go with him to the back of the line, and we go down the stairs, and hit the tunnel, and go down to the prison church again.

We're walk through the tunnels like we did the week before, and right before the door to the church, Jimmy grabs my arm and takes me up the stairs to a different door, and I follow him. This door has bars on it and it's usually locked, but this time it's wide open. We bust right on through it. We walk up a couple more wooden steps and open another door, and we're in the middle of the prison canteen and café, which is run by the low-risk inmates.

Jimmy just walks right in, like he's king shit. He goes up to this brunette who is working there, and he's kissing her, and she's kissing him back. He says, "We got to go." She takes off her apron and goes with us out the front door. Suddenly, we're free! And a lot of the other nuts in the canteen run right out there after us, yelling, "They're leaving!"

The road is right there. And guy with a 64 GTO convertible is sitting there with the engine running, and this guy starts honking the horn and revving the engine when he sees us. This guy was an ex-patient at the nuthouse who knew Jimmy and the girl, and she connected everything up. He was our ride out of there.

"I told you it'd probably work," the driver says.

I said, "Drive! Drive!"

Finally, he floors it, burns rubber, fish-tails out of there. We go out through the gate, he takes a hard left, and fish tails right into the ditch.

While we're in the ditch, the inmates have caught up with us, and I tell them to help push out of the ditch.

As we soon as we get the car out of the ditch, the other inmates

are trying to open the doors and jump into the convertible.

People are hanging onto the car, and we're pushing them off as we head out. We end up with nine people in the car, and they're giggling away!

We drive down the road a while, and the first night we spend out in the country in some farmer's field.

The next morning, it's cold out, and I'm thinking how are we going to get rid of these hangers-on. We all pile into the car, and we drive off. When we come to a wooden bridge, I say, "Now's a good time to stop and take a piss. Let's just do it here off the side of the bridge and we can all see each other."

I told Jimmy when everyone starts pissing, we should just

push them in.

It's only like a 10- or 15-foot drop. So we pushed four of them into the stream, and now we're down to five of us. We take off and leave the rest of them screaming in the water.

One of the guys in the car lives in Omaha and tells us that he's got money and food at his house, so we head over there. He runs in and about ten minutes later he comes running out of his house with a pillowcase and gets in the car. His family members are running after him, but we head out before they get to the car. He dumps out what's in the pillowcase in the back seat of the car. He's got a pot and a box of uncooked macaroni and cheese, and no less than three books of pennies that someone had been saving. His food and money turned out to be nothing. Now we're worried that our getaway car has been discovered so we tell the driver to drop us off at a friend of Jimmy's, who had a farm nearby, and that the driver needed to go, which he did.

At the farm, I called up my buddy John. He was several years older than me, and he had a wife and a kid. He had a connection through his brother, who was in Vietnam and was shipping drugs back to him. And he hooked him up with a connection in Lincoln who was selling psychedelics. We'd go to this guy's house. He had tie-dyed sheets hanging in his living room, so you had to walk through this maze of sheets just to get into his kitchen. In the kitchen, he laid out every sort of psychedelic you could think of.

John said he knew how to make some money by harvesting the hemp on the farm. At that time, weed was growing everywhere as a hemp crop. We'd go out and strip the weed out of the farmers' fields. We'd dry it up and brick it up. We made a press to brick the weed up. Four one-inch plates we welded together to make a box, and then we welded a hydraulic jack to the top plate and it would press the weed together into a brick.

One night, I called up Pops and told him where I was. He said he'd drop a bag off about a half mile from the farm. He put some baloney sandwiches and $100 in the bag, along with some clothes. So a couple hours later, I went out down the road and found the bag.

A few nights later, I snuck into town to see Pops and get more money, and on my way back, I was walking back down a dirt road, and this other farmer pulls up and asks me if I need a ride.

"Sure," I say.

"Never seen you before," he says. "You're not from around here, are you?"

"No, I'm just staying at this farm."

"Oh, yeah," he says. "They're a nice couple."

When I told the farmer about this, he said, "He's the nosiest fucker around. You shouldn't even have gotten into his truck."

A few days later, I'm up in the barn and everybody else is in the house. I'm just waking up, and I'm looking out the bale door and I can see off in the distance this trail of dust coming down the road. I can see that they're sheriff's cars.

"Hey, cops, cops! Cops are coming."

Hell's Angel's dude, he comes out, him and his wife.

"The sheriff's coming," I tell him.

He says, "You stay there."

The sheriff and his deputies pile out with guns drawn.

"Come out with your hands up!"

The farmer and his wife and his kid come out, and the sheriff says, "We're looking for a couple guys who escaped the nuthouse. We know that one's your friend, Jimmy, and this other guy is named Gerald."

"They're not here," the farmer says. "It's just me and my family."

"Well, this farmer picked this guy up, and he said he was staying here. I'm pretty sure it was your buddy Jimmy."

Jimmy hears this. He's up in the attic, hiding.

He yells out, "You'll never fucking take me. He has a 410 single-shot rifle. He sticks it out the window and shoots at the sheriff but misses.

"Oh, fuck, Jimmy!" I say to myself.

"Not here, huh?" the sheriff says, and runs into the house.

The deputies handcuff the farmer. And they drag Jimmy out with handcuffs, and he's squirming and screaming and wriggling around.

But they didn't find me in the loft. One deputy looked into the barn and didn't see anything and didn't bother to check where I was hiding.

After they left, the farmer's wife comes out and says, "You got to get the pot out of here, today!"

So I called John up, who drove over from Beatrice, about 20 miles away. Me and John put the pot in his car, a 56 Ford Victoria Slant 6. We took that shit to Boulder. It was lousy weed, but we'd get our hands on some good stuff, and we'd cut a two-inch hole out of the brick and put the good weed in the middle. When I was selling it, I'd chop it right down the middle in front of a customer to get to the good weed, and I'd roll one up for them to taste it, and they'd say, "That's really good weed."

In Boulder back then, then they had a one-block area around the campus called the Hill. There'd be just a mob of people walking around in a circle. Hundreds of people. One guy would be shouting, "Weed." Another would be hawking hash. And another would be selling cocaine. You couldn't do the deal right there in front of everybody, so if someone was interested, you'd go up in the mountains with them to take care of business there.

Then one day at the hotel in Colorado we got a knock on the door. We hid the weed under the mattress on the wood frame of the bed. I look out the window and there's this huge guy. He looks like a biker without a motorcycle. He had a beard and a baseball cap and he's wearing a leather vest. And I don't know who this guy is.

John says, "Check it out."

"I want some weed," the guy says.

"You must be at the wrong door," I say.

"No," he says, "I'm here to get some weed. I saw you selling some on campus."

"I don't know what you're talking about."

"Come on, dude, I know you got the weed. I saw you there on the Hill."

He was just talking and talking and talking.

"If you don't let me in, I'll just keep talking about it out here," and he raises his voice even louder.

John says, "Just let him in. Let him in."

So I did, and he plopped himself down on the chair, and he didn't move from that chair for the next three hours.

We tried and tried to get him out that door.

He said, "Why don't we just smoke some?"

I said, "Dude, we don't have any."

Finally, he gets up and says, "OK, I'll see you on the Hill."

I watched him out the window as he went into the parking lot, which was icy. All of sudden, he starts doing circles with his arms held out.

We were worried he was making a signal to somebody.

My buddy John said, "Let's leave the shit and go."

I said, "No, let's just wait."

But John insisted.

So we backed the car up to the motel door and loaded the weed into the trunk and on the back seats. We drove onto the campus, and just left the car there with all the weed in it, windows down, with the hopes that the college kids would take the weed and destroy all the evidence for us.

We walked back to the motel room, and we were no sooner in the room when the door just exploded.

It was the DEA, the federal narcs, and they found a little bit of hash in the pipe we had. So they hauled us off to the Boulder jail and transferred us to the big jail in Denver.

It was one of those, "fight or fuck" jails, where the bullies take the weaker ones out and say, "Suck me off, or I'll beat you down."

We only had enough money for bail for one of us. I said, "John, you got a wife and kid, you go back home. I'll ride this beef."

He got bailed out. And I was left there in jail.

This guy Frenchie comes at me. He tells me he wants me to suck him off.

I say, "Fuck you."

Then he wants to haggle with me.

"Why don't you just let me lay down on top of you with my clothes on, and I'll rub it up and down on top of you."

"You're not going to do any fucking shit to me at all," I tell him.

Fortunately, he backed off. He just came after me to see if I'd submit.

This was the mentality of the whole jail. And it was rampant across most jails and prisons: sexual bullying. You couldn't stand up for any kids who were being abused. Bullies have bully friends. If you interfere, you get in trouble. You might get your ass kicked.

I was in this jail for 120 days.

I got a public defender who was really aggressive. The DA was offering a plea agreement. And on the day of our court hearing, I told my lawyer, "You know what? I'm thinking of taking the deal."

He said, "No you're not. You're taking a bus home today."

In court, the public defender does his thing: "Your Honor,

they omitted this, and the police did this wrong and that wrong."

The judge buys it and says: "Case dismissed."

My attorney goes to the jail with me and makes sure I get processed right away because he says the DA is getting ready to refile charges and arrest me again, and also that there's a warrant for me from Nebraska.

I'm out the door in 15 minutes.

He hands me this bike, and says, "You got to get out of here as fast as you can."

I rode that 10-speed bike all the way from Denver to Boulder. I picked up my stuff and rode the bike to the bus station to get back to Nebraska.

When I got back home, the police were looking for me, and I was arrested for escaping. I go to court, and the judge offers me a deal. He'd give me an extra year, which was to run concurrently with my sentence for second-offense petty theft, on the condition that I join the Army when my sentence was completed. So I agreed. Since I had credit for time served, I had only had a little bit of time left.

When I finished my sentence, they vanned me to the parole office in downtown Omaha, and all these gang members were standing on the stairs shooting the shit. I had to walk right in between these guys, and they all recognized me from my time behind bars. They weren't my friends.

I go in and talk to the parole officer.

I say, "I just saw a bunch of the guys I was in prison with, and they're going to come after me."

"The bus station is only a block and a half away."

"I won't be able to make it that far."

"All I can do is give you a voucher for a bus ticket, Gerald, and wish you good luck."

So I come out of there with a voucher, start walking down the stairs, and there's no one on the stairs. For a second, I thought I was in the clear.

But when I open the door, they're lined up on both sides just waiting for me. So I shut the door and go back upstairs and tell the secretary that I need to use the phone to call a cab.

"Where you going?"

"Going to the bus station."

"It's just around the corner!"

"I know, but I still need a cab."

So she lets me call the cab, and I'm waiting on the second landing as I watch for the cab to pull up.

When it gets there, I run downstairs, fly out the door, and run in as fast as I can, grab the door handle, and jump in, and lock the door.

The guys rushed the cab as a I screamed at the driver: "Go, go, go!"

As he headed out, he passed the bus station before he asked me where I wanted to go.

"I'm going to the bus station!"

"It was just across the street."

"Did you see those guys?"

So we went around the block again, and they didn't follow us, luckily.

I gave the cab driver $20, which was a lot of money back then.

He was happy. And I was happy.

CHAPTER 6:

VIETNAM, 1967

It was 1967, and the Army sent me to Ft. Lewis, Washington, where I went through basic training and then AIT: Advanced Infantry Training.

Ft. Lewis is in a beautiful setting just outside of Tacoma. It's really green, and you can see the mountains.

When you first get there, they're yelling at you. They start conditioning you from jump street to move fast and do what you're told.

I didn't care for that. I didn't like being yelled at and told what to do all the time, right in my face. The hardest part about being in the military was swallowing your pride and taking orders from someone you don't know. I felt like I was in prison again.

Once we get to the barracks, they explain all these rules

and regulations. You can't walk in the middle of the floor in the room for some reason. Your footlocker has to be a certain way, your bed has to be done a certain way, and you need to be dressed a certain way, and if you don't have everything in order, they yell in your face and make you do P.T. It wasn't therapy but it was physical: a lot of pushups. Drop down and give me 50. Drop down and give me 100.

They always gave you more than you could ever do, and then you'd get penalized for not being able to do it.

We had a drill sergeant who, starting the first week, would come into our barracks between 2:00 and 3:00 a.m. drunk. He'd bring in his electric guitar and turn on all the lights and walk down the middle of the floor. He'd set the amp down, plug it in, and start playing rock and roll. Of course, we all had to wake up, though we didn't want to because in a couple hours, we had to get up anyway and do physical training.

After the first month, he started taking us outside and he would pair everybody off and say: "You're fighting him, and you're fighting him, and you're fighting him."

We'd have to bare-knuckle it and fight each other. All the other guys would stand around us in a circle and cheer us on.

He'd yell things like, "Get in there. Don't be a fucking pussy, you faggot!"

He became a drill sergeant after four tours in Vietnam. On his last tour, he had three VC prisoners in the helicopter tied up. One of them called him an American motherfucker in Vietnamese, so he kicked them all out of the helicopter and killed them. He was a lieutenant, and they busted him down to a sergeant and sent him back to the United States, and that was my drill sergeant. He was a little fucked up in the head.

He had a bunk and an office in the supply closet. He'd call a couple of us in there every once in a while, and he'd have a couple of drinks and a joint with us, and we'd all shoot the shit. One time when we were doing this, I was getting really high, and I thought everything he was saying was so funny that I started slapping him on his leg and yelling, "Stop, stop." He flips out and grabs me and throws me across the room. "Get the fuck out of here," he said, and I never went back there again.

The drill sergeant got busted down for his escapades while I was there. All the weed and the booze and waking us up in the middle of the night -- and even introducing us to a woman one night that he'd met at a bar --got him into trouble. He was crazy, but I kind of liked him.

During the week, we had regular physical training. We'd go on 5- or 10-mile marches, full packs. A lot of double-timing, which is basically running, in all kinds of weather. We did a lot of work in the rain. After a mile or two, we'd round a bend, and there'd be a couple of guys teargassing us, and we couldn't turn around. We had to keep going, with no masks on. We moved through it, and we got into this building, and we had to run through it. It's filled with teargas. You can't breathe. You're coughing. It's horrible.

Then we had the low-crawl, which is crawling through a field of sand and dirt and mud and sawdust and rocks, and right above it, about two feet, are lines of barbed wired. You've got to crawl under the barbed wire, and the whole time they're shooting tracer bullets over our heads. They tell us, "Don't stand up." One kid puts his hand up and says, "Stop, stop!" And he catches a bullet in his hand and starts screaming. The drill sergeant shouts at him, "Crawl, crawl!" And finally, he calls a ceasefire and attends to the kid.

After basic training, we had AIT. We trained with pugil sticks with padded ends on them. They taught us how to use the bayonet: Parry left, parry right. They taught us how to strike with the butt of the rifle.

By the way, we were never supposed to refer to our rifle as a gun. It was a sign of disrespect. And there was a chant that went along with this instruction: "This is my rifle, this is my gun (grab your dick), this is for killing, this for fun (grab dick again)."

If you ever dropped your rifle and it hit the ground, you had to do what's called "the dying cockroach." I had to do it once. You have to lie on your back with your feet and arms in the air, holding your rifle in the air, and you have to say, "I'm a dying cockroach, I'm a dying cockroach."

It's to teach you to never drop your rifle.

In AIT, you also have the Towers: These are like 15-foot wooden towers. You jump off of them to learn how to land and roll as if you were landing from a parachute jump.

I became friends with the corporal. We could get 3.2 beers on the base but nothing stronger, unless you were an officer. The only way you could hard stuff was to go to town, so one day he said, "Let's go out." He got me some clothes, but they were too small, and he brought me some shoes, but they were two sizes too small. I wore them anyway, and we went to town and got really drunk. We got busted coming back through the gate. The drill sergeant made me clean the tiles in the bathroom with a toothbrush for about a week.

After four months, they teach you how to pack your stuff up, they weigh you, and they put you on a big transport cargo plane. You land in Da Nang, and you get off on the tarmac, you line up in formation, and they march you to your barracks, which is nothing but an old Quonset hut.

Vietnam was hot and humid, and it rained a lot. And the air smelled, and the water smelled.

They put us through orientation for a week or two and told us what to expect: what's the vegetation like, and what animals and reptiles and poisons and plants we might encounter. They updated us on the war and what the goals were. They were like the coaches before the football game, getting us all hyped up.

Then they sent us out on patrol. They tell you where to go, and that's where you go.

I was pretty fucked up. I was doing heroin and smoking weed. Anything you wanted you could get dirt cheap there.

Then one day, I'm walking through the jungle with my boys, and I was high. We were on an animal trail, and this Viet Cong kid pops up, screaming and running at me. I raised my rifle to shoot him, but he ran right into my bayonet, with force that knocked me backwards. And while he was impaled on my bayonet, he started hitting my head with the butt of his rifle. But then he stopped and rolled over dead. He looked like a 12-year-old boy.

"Medic, medic," I yelled, because my neck was killing me.

He said, "Check in at the end of patrol," because we had to keep going. It wasn't safe there.

At the end of the patrol, I went to see the doctor, who did a quick X-ray.

"You got multiple cracks in your neck," he said.

"Did you ever have prior injuries to your neck?" he asked.

And I told him I'd broken my neck when I was 15 in a diving accident.

"They should have never taken you into the service," he said. "I'm sending you stateside. I've got to put you in a neck brace and take you to the hospital."

So off to the hospital we go. And they put me in a neck brace and fly me home to Fort Sam Houston, Texas. They put me in the hospital at the Fort, and the first week there I got spinal meningitis, hepatitis, and mononucleosis from the other patients – these were rampant in the hospital. Guys were just dropping dead. You'd joke with the guy in the bed next to you before you'd go to sleep at night, and by the next morning he'd be dead.

All they gave us was giant cans of Hi-C juice but no food for several days.

I was in the military hospital for a couple weeks, and I got an honorable discharge under medical conditions.

I served just short of six months. And that disqualified me for benefits because back then, they had a law on the books that you had to be an active service member for six months to get VA benefits. I was short by two weeks.

I get nothing. No pension. No back pay. No medical, nothing. I appealed this three times, but I got nowhere. It just sucked.

And I'm haunted by that kid I killed. I got no counseling for killing anybody. Sometimes if affects me really bad. I can't ever forget it.

CHAPTER 7:

CRICKET

From Fort Sam Houston, I got on a flight to Fort Lewis, Washington, for my discharge, and we had a layover at Buckley Airfield in Aurora, Colorado, for a couple hours. So I got off the plane and walked through the terminal and went outside to get a smoke. As I come out of the airport, there's this girl out there sitting in this Oldsmobile, and she waves at me and beckons me over to her car.

So I got to the passenger side window, and I bend down and ask her, "What's up?"

"I dropped a friend off," she says, and asks me whether I'm in the Service and whether I need a ride.

I had my uniform on, so it was kind of obvious, but I told her yeah, and I was there for just a couple hours.

"It's too bad you can't stay," she says. "I got a hotel room, and some pot and some booze."

So I think about it for all of two seconds, because I'm young, dumb, and full of cum, and I jump in the car.

"I'm Cricket."

"I'm Jerry."

"Please to meet you," she says.

She's driving barefoot and has short shorts on, and she takes me to this hotel. She opens the hotel room, and we go inside, and she rolls a joint, and we have a couple of Jack and Cokes. "All this is free," she says.

It wasn't long before we're having some great sex, and then we take a shower. We're drying off when the door opens and this guy walks in.

Cricket jumps up, runs over to him, gives him a big kiss, and turns around to me and says, "Jerry, this is my fiancé, Bob. Bob, this is Jerry. He just got out of the Army, and I met him at the airport, and he needed a ride."

Cricket made up a story for Bob, right there on the spot, telling him that I had a two- or three-day layover to wait for a certain Greyhound bus to take me back to San Francisco.

Bob bought the whole thing. He was friendly and docile. He was in love with Cricket, and she had him whipped.

"Wow, is there anything we can do to help you?" Bob asked.

Cricket jumped right in and said, "He needs a place to stay. Can't you get him a room here?"

And Bob, who it turns out was working at the hotel, said, "The hotel's full. It's the weekend. But we got two beds. You can just stay here. And I'm hardly ever in the room because

I'm working so much."

Cricket said, "That's a great idea!"

Bob even offered to comp me meals at the hotel, and Cricket asked him if it was all right if she took me shopping because all I had was my military clothes. He thought that was a good idea, too.

So I stayed there with them. And every time he'd go to work, we'd go to work. And if we felt like going out, she'd take me all over town. We'd go lie on a blanket by a lake. We'd go fuck in the woods. We'd even fuck while I was driving her car.

It got to the point where I was getting paranoid that Bob was going to find out, so I suggested we do something together. On his day off, we decided to go to the county fair, and we're riding the rides, and hitting the barbell. Bob and I were both being competitive, trying to throw the best darts to win a teddy bear for Cricket. We get to this pellet gun shooting contest, and they suggested since I'd been in the Army, I should easily win this stuffed bear for her. But I failed miserably because the sights weren't right. So Bob took his turn and won the fucking bear, which pissed me off. But we all got a laugh out of it. And actually I was starting to like Bob.

And the more I liked him, the more the paranoia turned to guilt. I knew I needed to end this thing before I broke up their relationship. But Cricket had different ideas. She wanted me to stay, and she told me one day after having sex that she loves me and that she's not in love with Bob, and she wants to break it off with him and be with me.

"Let's don't do that," I told her. "I got to leave and get back to my family in San Francisco."

But Cricket insisted, and a little while later, we had sex again, and in the heat of passion, she said, "Why don't we get married?"

Now she's got me pussy-whipped, so I said yes.

She told Bob, who broke down crying.

"Why? What did I do? I love you?" he kept saying.

She kept trying to console him. "Sometimes things just don't work out," she said, "and I didn't mean to fall in love with Jerry, but I did. Can't you just be happy for us?"

After a while, he calmed down, and he was such a helpful guy that he actually gave us a free room at the hotel.

A couple days later, we went down to the courthouse and got married. We picked up a witness in the hallway, and gave him $2, and went back to the hotel.

But we didn't want to stay at the hotel long, so Cricket said we should go to her mom's house. It was an old wooden two-story house that was all broken down. We go inside, and there are dogs running around, and it smells like urine and dog shit. Her mom was a big fat woman sitting in front of the TV smoking Pall Malls and drinking gin.

As we're walking through the living room, Cricket says, "Mom, this is Jerry," and we keep walking to the back bedroom, which was pretty clean and nice. We hung out there and smoked a joint.

She needed to tell her mom that she'd broken it off with Bob and married me, instead. She knew her mom would be mad because her mom wanted her to stop whoring around and marry Bob, who had a steady job.

So we went out into the living room, and her mom shut the TV off, and blurted out, "So who's this?"

And Cricket said, "Mom, this is my husband, Jerry. He's in the Army."

"You're going to fucking get it annulled," she told Cricket right away.

"No, I'm not," Cricket said. "I love him!"

"Well, he's not staying here," her mom said, and they yelled and screamed at each other for a while.

We stormed out of the house and drove around for a bit and had a couple drinks. Then we snuck back into her mom's house late that night.

The next morning, we got up and her mom was making pancakes for us. We're sitting there eating, and she says, "Well, what are your plans? What are you going to do for money? Do you have a job?"

Of course, all my answers were no. Her mom says, "You can stay here, but you're going to have to find a job."

"OK," I said.

I spent two or three days looking for work, but I couldn't find anything and I started to feel defeated, and my flight impulse kicked in.

It was real early in the morning, 4:30 a.m. or 5:00 a.m., the next day. There was snow on the ground, and I walked down to a coffee shop and called a cab. I had the cab take me to the bus station, where I bought a ticket to San Francisco and ghosted Cricket. So much for my first marriage.

CHAPTER 8:
WHITE BOY JERRY

My brother was in San Francisco and was living in a residence club called the Ansonia. I went there to visit him, and he helped me pay for a room for a month. At the Ansonia, there was a deal if you didn't have enough money for rent, you could work for your rent as a maid or a cook or a waiter or front-desk clerk. I decided to work in the kitchen and the laundry, while I looked for work outside.

I got a job at an import-export company that bought all this Chinese crap, like little dragons and figurines and fireworks and toys. My boss would sell bags of this stuff to people, and we'd box it up and mail it out. It was a shit job, but it got me down on Market Street, where everyone was a hustler. It would turn you into a hustler if you weren't one already, and of course, I already was one.

My co-worker was a Puerto Rican hustler named Marcos, who stood all of four feet eleven. His wife was a white chick named Lynnette, six feet tall and one donut short of 300 pounds. She was a nice gal, and they were in love, and I liked hanging around with them.

At work, Marcos and I would walk up and down Market Street on our breaks, and he knew everyone. He introduced me to his friends, and he'd go do a deal right in front of me. He'd give the guys some coke or hash or LSD, and then we'd move on down the street. He was making hundreds of dollars on a 15-minute break! I was impressed. He had the life I wanted, and I started making connections through him and gradually started doing my own deals.

I'd be walking around San Francisco barefoot, growing my hair long and wearing blue jean bellbottoms. I was handling my business, making money, selling drugs at a lot of places, including at the residence club. But not weed. I did a couple weed sales there, and it got back to the other person who was selling weed there. He came at me and told me that it's his turf and to stop fucking up his business. I said, "All right, but can I sell coke and acid here?" And he said, "Yeah, that's fine."

Once a month, the owners of the residence club would throw a party down in the basement. People would be sitting on the stairs, drinking and smoking weed and mingling. At one of these parties, I'm sitting in the corner of the basement, drunk and high. All of a sudden, this girl walks over to me, and sits down right next to me.

She says, "How you doing? I'm Deborah with an h!"

"How do you spell Debra with an h?"

"There's Debra, D-E-B-R-A, and there's Deborah, D-E-B-O-R-A-H, and that's how I spell it. I'm Jewish and I'm from Boston," though her accent had already given her away.

"I came out here with my girlfriend Jennifer. She's Jewish, too. We grew up together. We're best friends. Jennifer's sleeping with your brother, and she thought we should meet."

I was so drunk and out of it that all I heard, in my mind, was, "I think we should fuck."

I hugged her and stuck my tongue down her throat.

She says, "You want to go upstairs?"

I told her, "You got to help me." I was that drunk.

The residents were all making lude comments as we passed them by: "We know what you two are up to!"

We got up to her room, and Jennifer and my brother Don were in there. It was a little embarrassing, so they went up to Don's room.

We saw them later, and smiled at each other, knowingly.

Me and Debbie became an item. We went everywhere together, and we'd often spend weekends with Marcos and Lynnette at a house in Diamond Heights, which belonged to a friend of Debbie's. Out back it had this balcony overlooking a mountain covered with succulent plants. Early one evening, we're out there tripping on a thousand mics of orange sunshine and watching the sunset. Lynnette picks Marcos up and sets him up on the railing, and he turns around to look at the sunset and falls over backwards and hits the plants, which were still wet from the fog. He just zips down that mountain until he comes to a stop at a chain link fence at the bottom. We're scared shitless.

"You got to get him, you got to get him!" screams Lynnette.

We get in the car and go down the mountain a ways and park on the street near a million-dollar home, and we had to cross their property to get to Marcos. He was so fucked up! His face was all scratched and his body was bruised. We took him down to the clinic in the Mission District, and they patched him up and sent us home.

A few days later, we got together with a couple at the Ansonia, Mike and Kim. Mike was a privileged white kid who was there slumming. He just wanted to be with regular people instead of rich, snooty people who he grew up with. Kim was from India. They didn't seem to have much in common, except they were both pretty naïve. We'd go out to meals together, and he'd pay for them. I'd find some drugs, and he'd pay for them. And then we'd all do them. That was the arrangement, and it worked for me. We became friends.

So one day, I was walking around the city barefoot and no shirt on, and I came across this driveway that had a white Volkswagen van in it with a "for sale" sign on it. They only wanted $200 for the van. So I go up and knock on the door, and a woman comes out and tells me a story about buying the van for her son because he'd always dreamed about going on a cross-country trip in a VW van, but he died in a car wreck about six months before. They couldn't bring themselves to get rid of the van right away, but they were selling it now. So after she told me this story, I told her, "That's exactly what I want to buy it for. It's been my dream, too, to drive cross country." I was just trying to con her. She offered me a cup of coffee, so we went inside and she decided to sell me the van. I reached into my pockets, and I only had $90. I told her I'd give her the $90 right now, and I'd drive over and get the other $110 if she gave me the van. So I took the van and went to the Ansonia and called Mike and Kim and Debbie down.

"I got a surprise. I want to show you something," I said. So I showed them the van, and I told Mike I needed the $110, and that I wanted to take Debbie on a cross-country trip to Boston to meet her folks. He talked it over with Kim and they came back with a counter-offer: He'd give me the money as long as they could come with us on the trip. It was a deal.

We painted flowers on the outside of the van and outfitted it real nice. I even built a double-decker bed for us. And we had a great time going across country, until we got to Parsippany-Troy Hills, New Jersey.

I pulled into a crowded parking lot of a supermarket there, and the three of them went inside. I stayed in the van to pull out a syringe to shoot up some acid. While I'm doing it, I looked up and saw this guy peering into our window, so I pulled out the syringe. Next thing I know there's a knock on the door. It's a cop.

"What you doing?"

"Nothing."

"Why did you pick my car to check when there so many other cars here?"

"You're the only one driving a hippie van."

He pulls me out of the car and handcuffs me and then starts searching the car, pretty much tearing it apart.

At this point, Mike and Kim and Debbie come out of the supermarket and see what's going on. Mike's so green that he starts picking up stuff that the cop had taken out of the van and claiming it as his own.

"We're doing a search," said the cop. "You can't be picking stuff up."

They found LSD and some weed and my syringe and then took me to jail, letting the other three go.

I ended up one year in that jail for possession of LSD. I was the only prisoner in there most of the year. Overall, it was an easy place to be.

One thing that made it easy was that the sheriff's wife cooked for me! So I wasn't getting the usual slop, but real home-cooked meals. I liked the sheriff, too. He bought paint and let me paint the whole place. We got to be great friends.

On my last day, he drove me to the edge of town, and said, "This is how far I can take you. California is that way!"

I started to hitch hike, and a car pulls over.

"Where you going?"

"San Francisco."

"No shit. So am I. Get on in."

So I did. And he drove me all the way. He bought me food, and he gave me my own hotel room along the way. He was a high-roller.

When I got back to San Francisco, I went into a bar on Polk St. A guy was sitting there, and I ordered Jack and Coke.

"Put that on my tab," he said. "I'm Jimmy. I own the place."

They had live bands, big artists. It was a hopping place.

Through Jimmy, I met this Italian kid, Little Mario, at an Italian place across the street. We were doing cocaine and heroin in the dressing rooms at Jimmy's place.

It was quite a scene. There was another Italian guy there named Mike the Hat. He was an ex-boxer, who wore one of those little woolen English caps on his head. Jimmy let him sell all the cocaine he wanted at the bar, but no one else could.

Me and Mike the Hat became pretty good friends, and I'd sell coke for Mike and he'd pay me in coke.

I was getting in over my head here with my addictions, and it nearly cost me my life.

The first time I O.D.'d I was selling coke out of the Ansonia. One day I did a big blast of coke, and I was coked out of my ass. I took off outside with no shoes on and no shirt, and I walked barefoot all over San Francisco, almost to Daly City.

Now I don't know where the fuck I am, and I'm tired, so I grab a cab.

The cab driver is drinking a 40-ouncer in a brown paper sack. He sparks a joint, and shares it with me, and I offer him some coke, and we do a couple lines.

"Want to go to my hotel room on Lombard Avenue?" he asked. "I got some heroin there."

So we go there and do some heroin and coke. He says, "You can stay here, but I got to go make some money driving cab."

I've got a big bag of coke and new syringes, and I'm all alone, and that's a bad combination. So I fix myself a big blast of cocaine, about a gram of coke on the jar lid. I put some water on it, and it turned crystal clear: that's how clean and pure it was. I sucked this stuff up in a syringe and I'm thinking before I do this, "That's a lot of fucking coke, so I'm only going to push this halfway in." I tie off, stick the needle in my arm, pop a little blood, and then push it halfway in, and I stop. This immense rush, a tidal wave comes of euphoria, comes over me, then the euphoria turns to fear because I feel, as this is progressing, "I think I'm about to black out." The next thought in my crazy head is, "I got to hurry up and get the rest of this in before I pass out," so I pressed the plunger all the way in.

Everything goes black.

The next thing I know I'm waking up with the cab driver sitting on top of me, and he's slapping me, right hand, left hand, right hand, left hand. And he keeps screaming, "Breathe, in and out! Breathe!" And he's got ice packed all around me on the bed.

I wake up. "What happened?" I ask.

"You O.D.'d, and I've been working on you for about 10 minutes."

Not long after that, I O.D.'d again.

I'd rented a room at the Blue Hotel on Lombard Street, where the cab driver was staying.

One day, there's a knock on the door. It's the maid. She asks if I have enough towels or need anything.

"No, I'm fine for now," I say, "but you might want to check back later and give me some more towels."

I pull out a bag of coke, but this time I only put half a gram in the spoon and I put a little bit of heroin in there to make it a speedball.

I shoot it up, and I start nodding and scratching. I'm thinking, that's the heroin. But the feeling keeps intensifying. I'm thinking the heroin is getting stronger, but it's really the coke, and I turn into a rocket ship taking off again. I got this strange déjà vu feeling, with the euphoria kicking, and then the fear is coming back, and then everything goes black again.

Next thing I know, the paramedics are there!

They've got me on the bed, and the maid is standing in the background, and she's all scared and nervous.

Once again, I say, "What happened? What happened?"

The maid says, "I call ambulance! I come back with towels and you don't answer."

She saved my life.

The EMTs wanted to take me to the hospital, but I wouldn't let them.

"I'm fine," I said.

That same evening, I checked out of the hotel, and I gave the maid $100 as I was leaving.

But I didn't learn my lesson. This would be the story of so much of my life: I'd keep making the same mistakes over and over again. I'd keep surrounding myself with the same kind of people, doing stupid, criminal stuff.

Like stealing purses!

One place I'd do this was at the Holiday Inn on Van Ness Ave. I'd go to the bar at the Holiday Inn, and they'd have a live band every night. I'd look around and see which woman had a purse on the bar or at her table or on her chair.

After I picked my target out, I'd run and snatch and keep running out the door and down the hill, and I'd scoot into my neighborhood bar on Polk St, which was just a block away.

After a while, I polished my game. I started dressing up nice, and I'd walk over to some woman at the Holiday Inn bar and offer to buy her a drink. I'd talk to her and flirt, and then I'd wait till she had to go to the bathroom, and I'd say I'll watch your stuff, and then she'd go to the bathroom and I'd head out the door!

One day, there was this pretty woman who had slacks on and a low-cut blouse and business jacket. She told me she was from Santa Barbara and was just up here on a visit.

"I come here a lot," I said. "it's a really nice place." And we kept chatting together for a while, and I bought her a drink.

Finally, she says, "I got to go to the restroom. Will you watch my purse?"

"Sure," I said.

And she left, and I left.

I ran down the street as usual and got into the bar on Polk St, and opened up the purse and to my surprise, there was nothing there but two dollars, a .38 pistol, and a badge from the San Francisco police department.

"Oh, fuck, she was a cop," I said to myself.

I put the two bucks in my pocket and tucked the purse under my jacket and headed out of the bar. As soon as I'd opened the door, I saw that there were uniformed police officers coming out of the hotel and the nearby bagel shop.

I turn into an alley and dump the purse in the garbage

can there.

Then I come back out of the alley and the cops are on the corner, and the female cop is with them.

"Hey, can we talk to you for a second?"

The female cop says, "He's the guy who was at the bar with me. He's the guy who said he'd watch my purse."

I denied it. I said, "I'd just gotten nervous and up and left."

They searched me and didn't find the evidence, but they did find some cocaine.

They weren't buying my excuses, but what they were really concerned about was getting the .38 and the badge back.

So I played a little game with them: "Let's make believe that I might know where they are. Are you going to drop all the charges if you happen to find them?"

They huddled about it, but never gave me a commitment, so I didn't tell them where the weapon and the badge were.

They couldn't pin the theft on me, but they did book me on the cocaine possession. And they did get me on some of my previous purse snatches.

I did a little time for that, and when I got out, I started hanging out again with Mike and Mario at the Italian joint, and Mario introduced me to his brother Bill. Mario told me Bill was a big deal.

Mario would go on drug runs for Bill. He'd go to LA, lie on the beach, then pick up the drugs, and drive right back to San Francisco and hand them over to Bill.

Bill told me he could hook me up, too.

So I said, "All right."

Bill tells me I need to go down to San Diego and pick up four kilos and bring them right back.

"Here's the keys to the van," he says. "And don't stop anywhere. And don't touch the drugs. I'm sending someone with you to look after you."

I'm supposed to meet this person at the van at 6:00 a.m. I'm late. This beautiful blonde with skimpy clothes is there. She says, "I'm here to look after you." She tells me her boyfriend is a cop and is tied in with Bill, and they're all doing this together. He's on the payroll and so is she.

We drive straight down the coast and get to San Diego and get the drugs. By then, we're beat. She says, "Let's get a room." Thank God it had two beds.

We get up the next morning and while she's showering, I run out to the van, and open one of the kilos. I take a bit and then closed the bag up.

Near L.A., I ask her if she's ever been to the Whisky a Go Go?"

"No."

"You got to go."

I'd seen this billboard for Lynyrd Skynyrd playing there.

"Let's go see them."

"No, we probably shouldn't," she said. "I don't think that's a good idea."

But I convinced her. So we pull into the Whisky.

"You want to do a line?"

"No."

"Where did you get that?"

"I brought some."

So she does a line and I do a line. And we go into the Whisky.

We start partying all night with the musicians and anyone else who wanted a good time. The doors were wide open and everyone was smoking pot and snorting coke. One guy was walking around naked with a cowboy hat on.

We were so high and drunk we couldn't even go to sleep.

The sun comes up, and we start driving, hung over and all fucked up. We're going up the coast highway, and the cops light me up.

She's wearing a see-through crocheted bikini, and she asks me: "What are we going to do?"

"We're fine. We're fine."

I have a ball of cocaine and weed, and I put in my ass crack.

"You got a license?

"Yeah, I got a license."

"Can I look in your car?"

"Do you have a warrant?"

"I can get one, or I can get a dog. I can smell the weed. Open up."

"No, you need to get that warrant."

"Get on the curb."

And they handcuffed us both.

I said, "Can you give her something to cover up?"

Finally, the cop did.

"Why did you pull us over?" I asked.

 "You were driving funny."

I went to the Orange County jail. I was in there a total of nine hours. The charges were all dismissed.

So he gave me my keys back, but I was driving home alone because the girl had been released right away and was already back in San Francisco.

I drove straight back to San Francisco, parked the van in the designated parking lot, and left the keys where I was supposed to.

I called up Bill and told him I was back.

"All right. Talk to you later."

But he never talked to me again. They all shunned me.

So I went back to L.A. I didn't have a pot to piss in or a window to throw it out of. So I went down to the casino, where I met a friend of mine who lived nearby. He rented rooms to these old bums. I asked him if he had an extra room, and he said he did have one, and he'd be happy to rent it to me, only I didn't have any money. I told him I was good for the money, and I'd pay him within a week. The room I got had no windows in it, and it drove me crazy, so I left after a week.

I hustled some money, and I rented a nice little apartment. I bought all this furniture, including a waterbed, a wrap-around couch, a huge box TV, and a glass and chrome dining room table, with chairs to go with it. And there was a swimming pool at the apartment complex. Things were great.

I'd take cocaine and sell it to the white guys in the casino, where I was playing $1-$2 limit poker. I'd be waiting for someone to tap me on the shoulder. That was the signal for me to fold my hand and go to the bathroom with them and do the deal there. I was also selling drugs on the street corner, too. My crack house was an apartment right near the casino. We had an iron door with a little slot. You'd hand your money through the slot, and we'd give you the drugs through the slot.

Here's how we made our crack, if you really want to know. We had glass tubes about six-inches long and three-quarters of an inch in diameter, and we'd put two parts cocaine and one part baking soda in it, and we'd put a little water in it, and we had a pot of boiling water, and we'd stick the tube in the boiling water and start swirling it around clockwise and then stop. And we'd do it again, and you'd get a perfect crescent moon rock. Then you'd put the tube into cold water to solidify the rock. When it cooled down enough, you'd just dump it out.

I was the only white guy who could walk into Nickerson Gardens in Watts at midnight and get out of there alive. That's where the Bloods were. There was another housing complex called Imperial Courts a little distance away, and that's where the Crips were. And I was also welcome in there anytime. The police actually had a sub-station right there in the apartment complex where the Crips were.

I bought and sold drugs with both of them, the Bloods and the Crips. "White Boy Jerry," they called me. I foolishly had no fear.

They liked me 'cause I'd talk a lot of shit, and they knew I'd been in prison, and I'd become friends with some of them there.

You walk into this apartment and there's nothing but Black guys against the wall with high-powered weapons and some dude sitting on a chair with a scale on the table. You put your money on the table, he weighs out the stuff, and you don't say a word. No haggling. You just take it and go. The tension is so thick.

So I did this drug dealing for a while, until, one night, some guys pulled up next to me while I was leaving my apartment after I'd just rocked up three or four grams of crack and put them in plastic bags and went out into the street.

One guy is in the front seat, driving. The other guy's in the back seat.

The guy in the back seat says, "How ya doing, White Boy Jerry?"

So I ask him: "How you know me?"

They mention some guy's name I knew from the gangs.

"We just want to get some rocks," the guy in the back seat said. "We got $200 here. Why don't you get in the car?"

I was apprehensive, but I wanted the money, so I said all right, and I got in the back seat.

They started driving very fast down Vermont Ave, which is a six-lane road.

"Let me see the rocks," the guy in the back seat next to me said.

"Let me see some money," I said.

So then he pulled a gun on me, and a wave of fear washed over me.

"Now open your mouth," he said.

"What?"

"Open your fucking mouth."

And he shoved a pistol in it.

"Empty your pockets and put the stuff on the floor."

So I pull out my wallet and all the drugs I had on me.

"Is that everything?"

"Yeah."

"Pop that latch on the door."

I'm scared shitless at this point. I don't want to open that door.

"Pop that fucking latch," he said again, as he gashed the roof of my mouth with the sight of the gun.

Finally, I figured I better pop the latch and take my chances on the highway.

As so as soon as I opened the door, he kicked me out of the car onto highway.

I ball up and I roll and I roll and I roll, and I slide and I slide and I slide. I'm trying to come to a stop. And then I roll some more, and somehow I magically roll right up onto my feet. But I've lost my glasses by now, and all I can see is headlights coming at me. I dive off to the side of the road right before the cars come rushing by, and I land on the concrete curb, head and shoulder first.

I'm bleeding all over: my head, my shoulders, my legs. I'm a mess, looking like raw hamburger! I sit on the curb for ten or fifteen minutes trying to figure out just how badly hurt I am. I'm in shock because I felt no pain at that moment, and I'm mostly concerned about finding my glasses.

Finally, a prostitute named Chocolate comes along and says, "Jerry, are you all right?"

"I got to find my glasses," I say.

She doesn't say anything. She's just standing there staring at me. Soon she helps me walk back to the crack house. She gets some iodine to rub on my raw and bleeding skin, and it burns like hell.

I was very grateful to Chocolate for helping me out, even though I knew she was helping me probably because she just wanted to get some free crack. That was the beginning of us becoming friends.

It was also pretty much the end of my crack-selling days because I recognized now it was just too dangerous.

I'm not proud of those days. I'm especially haunted by getting this young Buddhist guy named David hooked on crack. David's father was a prominent professor in southern California, and his mother was music teacher.

I met David accidentally. He wasn't trying to buy crack from me. He was just trying to sell his yellow-colored Javelin, and the guy who wanted to buy it was living at my crack house. His name was John, and he lived there with his wife and two little girls.

When David came over to sell his car, he walked in and saw the steel door and the bags of crack, and he started asking all these questions. John didn't know how to answer him, so he called me in from the street and says, "There's a guy here with a bunch of questions – and a bunch of money." So I go up to the apartment and try to explain things to David, who is this little geeky guy with wire-rimmed glasses.

"The steel door is because we're selling crack here," I say. "And we have a crockpot full of oil, so in case the cops come, we can drop the drugs in there.

"Wow, this is fascinating," he says.

He tells us he's a devout Buddhist, and he says he goes to the Buddhist temple in L.A. regularly. To appear not so square, he tells us that he's smoked pot a couple times.

"This stuff is a little stronger than pot," I tell him. "I'll let you get one hit for free."

So he takes one hit, and he falls back in his chair and drops the pipe. His eyes are big as saucers and he's hyper-ventilating, and I'm worried he's going to have a heart attack. But he comes back out of it and jumps out of his chair, arms out, and turns around.

"What the fuck was that?" he asks. "Am I going to die? Am I OK?"

"You're all right, David. You're all right. That's how good it is. You want to go outside?"

"Yeah, let's go outside."

It's a beautiful, sunny day, and David says, "Wow, God wants me to smoke this!"

He was totally sprung – totally hooked on crack. This guy was so easily addicted it was scary.

We went back into the apartment, and he takes out some of the money he got from selling his car.

"It's $20 for a dove," I say, using the slang for a rock of crack.

"Can I smoke it here?"

"Sure," I say, and he smokes the entire rock.

Then he sists there staring at the carpet to see if there's any white pieces on it that he can smoke. He's what we call a "carpet sweeper."

So the rock's gone now.

"Give me some more," he says, as he takes out a $100 bill and asks, "What would that get me?

"That'll get you a whole gram," I tell him.

I give him the gram, and he sits there and smokes that whole fucking thing.

He throws down another $100 and says, "Give me another one."

"I'll give you another, but then you got to go, because these folks live here."

"OK, OK, I'll take one more hit and then I'll go."

He takes the hit, and I'm over by the door telling him to go.

"Wait a minute, wait a minute," he says.

He takes all his money out says, "I'll give you all this."

I say, "No, you got to go."

But John's wife says, "You can sleep on the couch," and she takes all the money.

He wakes up in the middle of the fucking night, and he's out of money and he's out of crack, and he wants some more.

"Look, I can go to the bank in the morning, first thing, I just need another hit," he says.

"OK, I'll trust you for $20."

"No, no, I need a gram."

So I give him a gram, and say, "You better make that last now because I'm not giving you anymore."

It's five in the morning, the coke's all gone, and David says, "You going to front me another one?"

e flowerpots full of incense. There are no chairs
ust pillows for you to sit on.

ks in and grabs a stick of incense and lights it off
me and sticks it in one of the flower pots with the
e does a bow and a Buddhist prayer and explains
e monks will come out and chant and pray.

g I know, David's taken his crack pipe out and

what the fuck? You're going to smoke that in the
"

noke because I'm here to ask for forgiveness. It's
e thing I'll ask for forgiveness for."

and I leave and wait outside for David, who comes
n minutes later, carrying a couple sticks of incense,
tation bells that were on the stage, along with a

those aren't yours," I say.

hing in there belongs to everybody," he says.

t in there to pray, and he ended up smoking crack
g stuff.

back to his place, and I watch him while he smokes
k. I'm trying to talk to him about quitting.

do you want me to quit? I'm your best customer!"

fuck you. I'll never sell you another rock again."

showed up again about a week or two later. He had
k of crack, about an ounce, the size of a tennis ball,
ch of powder cocaine and some baking soda. He
e to teach him how to cook it up in exchange for

"No."

"I'm going to go to the bank, and I'll come back," he says.

"No, you're not! You're not going anywhere," I tell him. "Don't think you're going to run out the door. Just stay here, we'll go to the bank together."

"Ok, well, give me another gram then."

So I give him another, and he smokes that up.

We drive to the bank and sit in the parking lot before it opens. I'm smoking a joint, and I sell him my crack pipe, and he keeps hitting the empty chore boy (the steel wool mesh of wire that serves as the screen on the glass pipe) to get at any of the remains.

"Put the pipe down," I tell him. "Quit that!"

Finally, the bank opens, so we go in, and David's being real short and aggressive with the teller. At one point, he says, "Look, it's my money. I can take as much as I want." He succeeds in withdrawing a couple thousand dollars.

We get out to the parking lot, and he starts throwing hundred-dollar bills at me.

"David, you're going overboard here," I tell him.

"Just give me the two rocks and I'll go home."

We go back to the apartment, and I give him the two grams, and I tell him he's got to leave.

Then he pulls his pipe out and says, "Let me get one hit for the road."

"No, you gotta go."

He walks out the door onto the walkway, lighting his pipe in public. He stops three or four doors down and leans against the railing.

So I go out and walk him all the way out of the apartment complex.

I don't have a car at this point, and he just sold his car, so I told him to call a cab.

"No, I'm going to need the money," he says.

"Well, take a bus home then."

So he leaves.

A whole day goes by, and I don't hear from him.

Finally, he shows up. He's driving his parents' van.

"I need some more," he says.

I sell him a gram.

He wants another.

"You gotta go, man," I told him.

So he goes down to his van in the back of the apartment complex, and he's smoking crack in his van. He's got the door open and the music playing.

Someone must have called the cops on him, because pretty soon the cops pull up and go over to his van. He's standing outside his van talking to the cops, and I'm thinking, "He's going to jail."

The cops pat him down and look into the van but find nothing at all.

Fortunately, he'd just finished off the last of the crack and dropped the pipe, stepped on it, and kicked it under the van.

So they let him go, and he came back up and said, "I need another pipe."

I took him to the head shop, and he bought a couple pipes

---

and came back to the a

"You can't smoke i
too much heat."

So he spent four day

At some point after

"David, you got to st
nice, friendly guy who'd
an agitated crackhead."

But he doesn't want t

I'm trying to become
dealer.

"Where do you live?" I

He lives upstairs in his
there. His room has got tar
guitar and a drumset, and s

He sits down on his bec
the crack, and he tells me ag

"How does the teaching
go hand in hand?"

"Well, they don't."

"So how do you deal with

"I go to the temple and asl
and I do yoga."

"Where's the temple at? C

"Yeah, let's go right now."

"Is it open?"

"Yeah, it's always open."

It's one of the big Buddhist

stage, there ar
on the floor, j

David wa
the eternal fla
other ones. H
to me how th

Next thin
is smoking it

"David,
temple here

"I can sr
just one mo

I get up
out about te
a few medi
prayer rug.

"David,
"Every
He wer
and stealin
We go
all his cra
"Why
"Well,
David
a big chu
and a bu
wanted n

some of his crack or some money. He'd found another guy to sell him crack, but the guy was charging him twice as much as I was, he said.

So, for $500, I took him to the kitchen and showed him how to make it, and then he tried it. He fucked up the first couple times but then finally got it right and was real proud of himself.

Then one night, six months later, he calls me up and tells me he needs my help, and can I come over to his house.

I go over, and one of his eyes is puffed up and there are scratches on his face and his arms are all bruised, and he can hardly walk.

"What the fuck happened, David?"

"I was buying some powder from another dealer, and they set me up. They told me they'd sell me $5,000 worth of powder, so I drove over to his house, and when I walked in, and I saw a bunch of other gangbangers there. They jumped me and beat the shit out of me."

I have to drive him to the emergency room at UCLA hospital. They give him a couple stitches on his legs and arms, and they cleaned up his scratches and gave him ice for his eye. They also tell him not to go to sleep right away.

"I'm going to quit smoking crack," he vows on the way home.

"And I'm not going to sell you any more crack," I tell him.

Over the next several months, we started hanging out and playing poker at the casino. We'd smoke pot together once in a while.

And after I got robbed and beat up and thrown out of that car, I told him I'm shutting down the crack house and he asked me if I had any rocks left.

I wanted to get rid of my inventory so I said, "Sure, as long as you're sure you can handle it."

I sprung him again. He goes home and gets caught by his parents smoking crack up in his room. They call the police on him. He gets arrested, and they said they wanted him sent to rehab.

I felt bad. He'd been on the road to recovery. He'd confessed to his parents about his drug use, and he'd started to go to NA meetings, and I derailed him.

I talked to his dad, who reached out to me and asked me to never see his son again and never sell him anything again. We actually had coffee one day – his dad and me. He didn't scream at me. He was surprisingly calm.

I told him I tried to get David to stop.

"But you were selling the stuff to him," he said.

What he was saying was true. If it wasn't for me, his son would be OK. He'd be chanting at the Buddhist Temple and still have his money in the bank. I just ruined that kid.

CHAPTER 9:
SCANDALIZING

Since selling drugs was getting too dangerous, I needed to find another way to make money, and I had a friend named Allen who had a money-making operation that he let me in on. Basically, it involved cashing bad checks at banks.

We called it "scandalizing."

Allen had all kinds of checks: cashier's checks, payroll checks, personal checks. He paid junkies and petty thieves to grab checks from any houses, cars, or businesses that they were robbing. So he had tons of checks, and he had a check protector that could print out any amount on the checks.

I worked with a crew: two girls, me, Allen. Whenever we were going to do a job, we'd get dressed to the nines. Before we'd go to the bank, we'd have all our paperwork in order. We'd make a check out for an odd amount, like $9,642, and then we'd fill out a deposit slip for that amount. The check that we were depositing was from one of the stolen checkbooks that Allen had acquired from some junkies, and the check we were cashing was drawn on the bank we were going to. We also brought checks with us that we were going to cash once we'd made that initial deposit.

So the scam began when I'd go up to the teller and give her the deposit slip and the check, and she'd hand me the receipt for it. And then she'd ask me: "Is there anything else I can do for you?"

"Yes," I'd say, and I'd pull out the next check for something like $3,241 and ask to cash everything but $1,000 of it, which I said I wanted deposited into the account as well.

Then I took out a third check for about $2,000, which I told her I needed as petty cash for the office.

I'm trying to keep her distracted and busy so she's not suspicious and so she's doesn't ask for my ID. I had a slip of paper with the denominations I wanted for all this cash: how many hundreds, how many twenties, how many tens, etc.

She'd stamp the checks, count the money, and hand it over to me.

It was that easy!

And here's how we got the account numbers for depositing the checks. We'd go to a grocery store and pick up the free fliers they had there for ads for the store. We'd grab three or four hundred of them. We'd drive down the streets in fancy neighborhoods and put fliers in every mailbox. But what we were really doing was seeing if any of the mailboxes had their flags up. That usually meant that the people who lived there were paying their bills. So in one smooth motion, we'd put the flier in and we'd grab those envelopes, and find their bank accounts inside on the checks they were mailing out. And once we had their bank accounts, we'd go to their bank the very next day.

I did that for a while and was making enough money to buy me a Lincoln Continental. I started playing poker at the clubs and selling drugs and doing forgeries on my own. I also met a couple girls who'd just got out of jail who were prostitutes, and I started running them out of a hotel on Normandy Avenue. I was making enough money that way that I didn't have to do the bank scam any more, even though my old partner would come by occasionally and try to get me back in the game.

He'd send the two girls who were part of our old crew up to see me. And they would plead with me: "Come back and work for us again."

But I didn't want to keep doing that because I was in full pimp mode by then.

A week or so later, one of the girls came over with her bag and said she'd left him.

I go, "He knows where I live. So we're going to have to move." I didn't want him to bring any heat on me.

Twenty minutes after she got there, he popped up. He had no weapon on him. But he had his keys in between his knuckles, and bam, he kept hitting me over and over again.

"Where is she? Where is she?"

She came out, and he grabbed her by the arm and threw her down the stairs.

That was the end of that.

I got kicked out of the hotel two or three days later, and everything started falling apart.

I got my ass handed to me by some guy. And other pimps started moving in.

"How you doing? I can take care of your girls if you want," one of them said.

I said no. But the girls heard it all, so they knew they had an option.

These girls saw it as some kind of weakness in me, and one of them, Natalie, did leave, and then after another week or so the other one, Coco, went to jail for soliciting a cop.

I had nothing left, except a raging heroin addiction.

So I started passing bad checks on my own. And it was paying off. I had a nice house, a waterbed, and a big-assed color TV.

But I finally got busted.

Here's how it happened: When I presented my check to the teller, she said, "That's not your account, sir." Turns out she knew the wife of the guy whose account it was!

I tried to grab the check back, and then I said, "Fuck it!" And I turned around to leave, but there were two cops there in the back, so I got arrested. I learned later that I'd been flagged. The banks had been sending in info about my MO. They were on the lookout for me.

They charged me with forgery, fraud, and "uttering a false instrument" — basically cashing a bad check – and they had a lot of evidence from a lot banks.

During their investigation, the D.A. hired a handwriting expert who proved that it was my writing on the checks. The expert also said that my handwriting showed that I had "an outgoing personality, a need to be noticed, and that I demanded attention." That's not an optimal characteristic to have for a criminal trying to avoid the police.

I made a deal that they would combine charges from the ones they knew about into one charge.

So I pleaded guilty, and was sentenced to prison for two years.

CHAPTER 10:
TWO DECADES
IN AND OUT

For the next couple of decades, I was in and out a lot of jails and prisons in California.

I'd be sent away for a year or 16 months or two years, and then I'd get out, and I'd start doing the same thing with the same people again, and I'd get caught again and go back in.

Occasionally, I'd get a legit job. But I had gotten back into heroin and selling drugs and writing bad checks and running whores. That's what I knew. But it wasn't a good plan for staying on the outside. I was wasting my life, and I didn't really care. That's how bad off I was.

I became very familiar with the California State Prison system. And the more time I spent in it, the more I realized that the system wasn't about rehabilitation. It was about sadism. And it was, essentially, a school for criminality. We all learned from each other about how to hustle.

I also understood that prison is different for Black folks. Most of the guards are white, and at least 70 to 80 percent of the inmates are Black. You stand back and watch, you see these guards act so superior over Black inmates. They'd scream and yell at a Black inmate for hardly doing a thing. If a white inmate had done the same thing, they'd barely say a word. They treated Black inmates like animals.

They do have Black guards, but they just stand back and don't say anything because they might need the white guards to help them sometime if the prisoners are coming after them.

And if there's a fight between a white guy and a Black guy, nine out of ten times, they're going to pound the Black guy and just handcuff the white guy.

———

Now I'm not going to go into detail about each and every state prison I was in. I was in a lot of them. But here are a few highlights, or lowlights, depending on your perspective.

The first place I went to was the Chino State Prison for intake. That's where everyone goes for intake. So I was there a lot. One time when I came back, they put me to work at the intake desk. I'd be typing away as the prisoners in their underwear told me their names and where they were from.

I met Ike Turner there. I took his intake. He couldn't read

or write. But he was great with numbers and mathematical questions. He was the life of the party at Chino. Everyone gathered around him, and he talked a mile a minute about him and Tina. Every month, a beautiful woman would visit Ike, and they would let him meet her not in the visitor's room but at the picnic table outside, where the guards usually ate, right next to the parking lot. We all thought it was Tina coming to visit but we couldn't be sure. But we were jealous that he could have a visitor outside.

———

At the state prison in Vacaville, I went to school, and I got my GED there. Turns out that Charles Manson was also in Vacaville at the time, and he was in school too. I never thought he was the school type. Anyway, as I'm coming out of a classroom one day and am heading into the next one, I see this commotion on the stairs. Two guys are stabbing Manson, and he falls right at my feet, blood everywhere, lying there face down. I stand against the wall as the guards come in. They ask everybody there, one by one, what we saw.

"Let me see your hands," they say, and they strip-search us all looking for weapons and seeing if we have blood on us. Eventually, they catch the guys and find the weapons.

I wasn't surprised by the attack. Everybody just hated Manson. Someone would always say, "I'd like to kill that son of a bitch." They locked him up after he got out of the hospital. They put him in protective custody. He was never in the main line again.

————

I was in San Francisco City Prison one time. It's an old, old jail, downtown. One day, an assistant DA in a suit comes up to my cell and tells me, "I got a call from your brother, who told me that your dad passed away." And he handed me a message from my brother, which said that Pops died of a heart attack, and he told me when the funeral was going to be. My brother also submitted a request to allow me to attend the funeral.

At that moment, I lost it completely and sunk back into the cell. Two gay inmates came by and consoled me, telling me they'd lost loved ones, too, which I appreciated.

Three days had gone by and I hadn't heard anything.

"Any word on me getting to go to my dad's funeral," I'd ask the guards. But I never got an answer, other than, "I don't know anything about it."

There were two avenues of thought among my fellow inmates: Either I was going to be able to go, or there's no fucking way you're going to your dad's funeral.

The doubters were right. I wasn't able to attend.

I went off! I started throwing cups of piss at the guards, and screaming and yelling at them, and threatening to kill them. I was just fucking raging!

So they put me in the hole for six months.

————

One place I was sent to was the old Santa Rita Jail. The U.S. government had a concentration camp there for Japanese Americans during World War II. The cells were five feet wide, five feet long, and five feet high. On top of the cells there was heavy gauge wire fencing, and a catwalk for the guards to look down on us. The doors of the cells were solid. There were no bars or windows, only the wire on the ceiling. I couldn't stand up in my cell without hitting my head. I couldn't stretch out in my bed. It was awful.

I was one of only two white guys in the jail at the time, and the rest of the inmates were all Black. We both had Black cellies, and because he became friends with this cellie, he thought it was OK for him to act Black and use the "N" word. It wasn't. He got the shit beat out of him. He was beaten up so bad one time that a Black guard brought him to my cell and put us together in the hallway and said, "Gerald, talk to him. Straighten him out. Put some sense into him. Tell him to start acting right." The whole side of his head was messed up, and one eye was closed.

"What should I do, Gerald? What should I do?"

"Keep your mouth shut," I said, "and quit trying to act Black. You ain't Black."

The guard laughed at that one.

But the inmate didn't change his ways, and eventually his cellie killed him. The story I heard was that the shot-caller, the leader of the gang in the jail, told the white guy's cellie to take care of him, or else.

———

Soledad was a very rough prison. Fortunately, my cellie, Toby Disney, was a really nice guy. He was from Oildale, California, and it's famous for two things: motorcycle gangs and meth. Toby was a biker, and some of these guys were pretty hard-core. They loved their fucking speed, and they were my friends. I was part of their clique. It's good to be in a clique in prison. Otherwise you're standing all alone.

The yard is huge at Soledad. It's the length of two football fields. And a lot of the inmates had hand-made weapons that they hid in the gopher holes in the yard. One time, a group of about 100 whites on one side ran at a group of 100 Blacks on the other, and many on both sides had weapons from the gopher holes or weights or anything they could get their hands on. They just started running at each other, like it was war. The guards in the towers started shooting off their guns. A couple inmates got shot, and one guard got hit in the foot. Mini-14s aren't designed for long-rage accuracy.

We had a lot of lockdowns at Soledad. One day when we were in lockdown, Toby showed me this ball of speed he had. He started snorting the shit and was bouncing off the walls. He gave me some, and even though I hated speed, I took it anyway. Then we got out of lockdown, and he spread it to all his buddies. And they were acting crazier than usual.

The most hardcore guy decided he didn't like something the guard asked him to do, so he attacked the guard, and other guards came down, and there was a big fight as other inmates joined in. On the third floor was a guard with a mini-14. He points the rifle at us, and one of the inmates sneaks up beside him and grabs the rifle from him. Soon the inmates had the guards all tied up. They threw all the mattresses outside the doors in a pile to try to block any bullets that might come. One inmate was behind the mattresses with the door cracked open with the mini-14. He was on watch.

The next day, the police come out with bullhorns.

"You guys got to come out," they yelled.

One of the inmates asked me what we should do.

"We probably should just come out," I said.

We didn't have any food, any water. They'd shut everything off. We were eating crackers and tuna fish and sardines -- whatever we had left. Speed and coffee.

The next day, the speed just ran out, and the inmates gave up. Half of them were still sleeping. It's called crashing for a reason.

Anyone who had any altercation with the guards went to the hole and got recharged. One got a kidnapping charge.

Toby and I weren't directly involved, so nothing happened to us.

But something did happen to Toby later -- not from a guard but from an inmate.

Toby was sitting down in the day room playing cards, and this guy comes up to the cell and says, "Toby told me to get that Guns N' Roses tape."

"Well, let me ask Toby down there," I say, and yell out to him.

Toby gave me the thumbs down.

So the guy goes to the day room a couple minutes later with a rock the size of a baseball. And he just whacks Toby in

Gerald Heckathorn

the back of his head. Blood spurts all over the place, and Toby has to go to the hospital to get stitches. After that, Toby lost a little self-confidence.

I got beat up a couple times, too, at Soledad.

One time this guy comes up to me and says, "Give me some weed."

"I'm not giving you shit."

He popped me right in the mouth.

I walked back onto the yard. He says, "What about now?"

I said, "I'm not giving you shit."

Motherfucker hit me again. But he got caught and was sent to the hole.

I had one other altercation there. I had a lot of money on the books, so this guy comes up to me and says: 'Can I have $1,500 to buy some heroin, and I'll share it with you?"

I give it to him, but he never gives me any of the heroin.

So I sharpened up my shank. I knew this guy's routine. He'd go jogging every day around the track.

One day he jogs on past me, and I pull out my shank and stab him in the ass, and then I go back to my cell.

"Gerald, was that you who cut him?" my friends would ask.

"I don't know what you're talking about."

And they'd laugh.

Prison: You either got your ass kicked or you fight back.

———

I had a surprise visit one day. I was doing time for some drug

118

charge or other in Soledad.

A lot of inmates, when they get in, they make out a visitor's list, and they put everyone's name down that they can think of: family, friends, anybody. But I never did that. I wanted to alienate myself from my family, and I didn't want to drag them into my criminal life like I'd done with Pops.

Out of the blue, I got a letter from one of my half-sisters. You see, my mom had two daughters from later affairs, Laurie and Shelly, and it was Laurie who sent me the letter. She's the glue that tries to keep the family together.

I'm a very emotional person, and I didn't expect to hear from them, so when I opened the letter, I started sweating and my ears got hot and my face turned red and my heart started to beat faster. I ripped the letter open.

In the letter, she asked me if I'd accepted Jesus Christ as my Lord and Savior and asked me if she, Shelly, and Mom could come up to visit me. It finally made me feel like there's someone out there who gave a fuck about me.

I wrote her back and told her I'd put them on the visitor's list, and that they should come on up in a couple weeks. And from that moment on the anticipation was so strong that I had trouble sleeping, and I walked around with a smile on my face. I couldn't wait to see them!

Two weeks later, the guard comes to my cell and says, "You've got visitors." So he took me to the visitor's room.

And there was my mom and Laurie and Shelly.

I got all heated up and flush and weird. I didn't know what to say to them. I felt guilty. Then we started talking, and my sisters told me how Mama just found God, and she told me all the benefits she received from finding God.

I was holding my mom's hands, and saying, "Yeah, I feel that, too. Can you put $100 on my books?"

I was being a jerk. The con was still in me, and I wasn't really feeling it. I was faking it. I'm trying to get money, and she's trying to save me.

After about an hour, they're getting ready to leave, and they want to pray one last time. So we all grab hands and my sisters started praying. This time, I started actually feeling something, and I was filled with the Holy Spirit. I'm not kidding you here. A warm, safe, peaceful feeling washed over me. After the prayers, we all hugged and said goodbye. It was a great visit, and a pivotal moment for me.

I went back to my cell and everyone's got a bible, so I took my little bible out and I started to read it.

In the days and weeks following their visit, my mom and my sisters would write me the nicest letters, and they kept filling me with the Spirit. I wrote them back, complaining at first about conditions in prison but gradually my attitude improved because of all the positive things they were writing to me. They encouraged me not to give up. They assured me that I could turn my life around. And they stressed the spiritual connection. I really looked forward to getting their letters.

I was getting letters from Mom once or twice a week. Then there was a two-week period where I got nothing from anybody. And then finally one Saturday morning, on Store Day, I was out in the yard, standing in line, waiting to order my stuff. And a couple guards walk up to me and tell me to step out of line.

"I've been standing here for an hour," I said. "I'm not getting out of line."

The bigger guard put his arm on my shoulder gently, and said, softly, "Gerald, you're going to want to come with me to the warden's office."

This was unusual so I didn't resist, and I instantly started to wonder what it was about, hoping that I was going to get released early but also worried that something bad might have happened.

He took me to the warden's office, and the warden told me to have a seat.

"Gerald, I got some bad news for you," he said. "Your sister Laurie called and informed us that your mother passed away."

The warden was trying to console me. "Sit there and take as long as you need," he said, as I sat there crying like a little girl.

He gave me some tissues and some water. I was in there like 15 or 20 minutes.

A secretary came in and asked me if I felt like harming myself.

I said, no, of course not.

I asked the warden if he knew when the funeral was.

He said no, but that my sister would contact me about it.

I asked him if I could go to the funeral. He said I should submit a written request and we'll see what we could do. So I did that.

Five days go by and I didn't get a letter from my sister. Finally, I signed up to make a phone call to my sister. They have these blue phones you use that look like payphones. So I called her up, and she tells me she wrote me a letter the same day she called the warden. In that letter, she had the information about when the funeral was, and a good part of the letter was to the warden, urging him to let me attend the funeral since we'd gotten close.

The letter should have been there days ago, so I asked her, when is the funeral.

"It was yesterday," she told me.

I was really pissed and very sad, swinging back and forth between the two. I shot a kite to the warden, telling him about missing the funeral and not ever getting the letter from my sister. The next day, the letter came.

So much for the warden's good intentions. I hated the fucking warden after that.

———

CMC, the California's Men's Colony in San Luis Obispo, is the prettiest prison I've ever been in. It's right on the ocean. And there's a golf course on the other side. It's a nice place.

But being a smart ass, I couldn't help myself from wising off to the intake officer, who asked, "Do you think that if you killed yourself that'd solve your problems?" I knew they were just doing a psych eval, but it struck me as such a stupid question that I said, "Let's see now: If I was dead, I wouldn't be sitting here in this jail facing all these charges and looking at the rest of my life behind bars. Yep, I think being dead would solve all my problems." I didn't give a fuck at that point, so I thought I might as well have fun with the intake officer.

He wasn't amused. They took me right to a padded cell at the state nuthouse in Atascadero and put me in a strait jacket for 24 hours for observation.

When they came in to reevaluate with me, I told them, "I was just kidding. Of course, I don't want to die."

I was in the nuthouse for 30 days, and when I returned to San Luis Obispo, I settled in.

But as much as I liked the place, I still got roughed up in there.

I'm walking back to my cell with my groceries, and this big white guy named Daley comes over and says: "Give me all your groceries, or I'll fuck you up."

"I ain't giving you shit," I said.

Then he knocked me out. I was kind of dazed when I came to, and just went back to my cell, and asked to be allowed in. The guard said you'll have to wait until mealtime's over. So I had to stand there and wait.

About a week later, Daley took my groceries a second time.

"I'm not doing that again. Fuck that," I said, and vowed to get back at him the next time.

But before Daley tried again, he got moved out for doing something even worse to somebody else.

———

The worst prison I was in was Corcoran. It's a maximum-security prison, and they had just built it when I arrived. I opened that prison! They needed inmates to go live there, and clean up the welding dust, which stunk like something burnt. We had to bring in the mattresses and get the cells ready and put all the finishing touches on the place. Then they started bringing in all the hard-core inmates, and we're waiting to leave. But we got stuck there for like six months.

Most of the inmates were there for murder or killing other inmates. There were serial killers in there. The worst of the worst. Rapists and pedophiles, too. There was one entire section for them. They had to be separated from the rest because otherwise they'd be killed.

The guards used different kinds of torture on the inmates. For instance, if you got into trouble, they made you take off your clothes and get into scalding hot water. Then they'd use hard-bristle scrub brushes all over your body, cutting you up. It was called "the bath."

I never got put in the bath, but I saw the result. It wasn't pretty. They treated people real bad there.

I just stayed to myself and kept a low profile. I didn't talk to anyone hardly. I just kept my head down. And no wise-cracking. I saw other guys make wisecracks, and they just got smacked.

———

In between my prison stints, I got married for a second time. (My first marriage had gotten annulled because we weren't married more than six months, and my mother-in-law insisted on it. She didn't like me.)

My second wife's name was Belinda Inez Mathews.

Here's how we met: I was driving taxi in Santa Ana, California, and I got a call to a bar downtown one night. So I walk in the bar and yell, "Taxi!" The bartender puts her hand up, and it's this beautiful big-titted Amazon woman with jet-black hair, and says, "Over here!"

So I went over there, and the bartender points to this little girl at the end of the bar. I'm still looking at this knockout bartender, and I keep flirting with her. The girl I'm picking up says, "I just got this drink."

"That's fine, don't worry," I said, and I ordered a Jack and Coke from the bartender, who I was lusting after, and she was flirting back.

The bartender introduces me to the girl who called the cab.

"This is Belinda, my friend from Arkansas."

I said, "That's nice," and kept after the bartender.

Belinda finished her drink and said, "I'm ready to go when you all are," in this thick Southern drawl.

"You talk funny," I said.

"No, you talk funny."

The bartender told me that she and Belinda were living in the same apartment with the bartender's mom.

When we were getting ready to go, I saw that Belinda was using a crutch, and I noticed she had a broken leg. I also noticed her short shorts and her tube top and her frizzy hair.

"She's precious cargo," the bartender said. "You take care of her. You kids go and have fun."

So I help her into the front seat, and I put her crutches in the back. As I'm driving her home, we're talking, and I'm getting to know her a little. And that Southern drawl is making my dick harder than penitentiary steel.

I helped her up to the door of her apartment, and she asked me if I wanted to come in and smoke a joint.

Of course, I said yes.

The bartender's mom, also a goddess, let us in. Belinda says, "I invited him in to smoke a joint."

The mom says, "You two have fun," and goes to her bedroom.

Belinda says, "What do you want to do?"

"I think you know what I want to do."

And we went to pound town right there on the couch, cast on her leg and all.

From then on, we kept going out. She'd ride in the passenger seat of the cab while I was doing my shifts. We got very close, and we'd take fuck breaks in the back of the cab.

We were falling in love over the next three or four months, and we got engaged. But in the middle I had to go to jail for 30 days for a simple marijuana offense at the Orange County Jail.

From the roof of the Orange County Jail, I could see Belinda's apartment one block away. And she'd climb on the rooftop of her apartment and put up signs saying, "I love you." And we'd wave back and forth. The other inmates teased me about this, and kept telling me she was fucking my roommate.

When I got out of jail and came home, I was paranoid that she was fucking my roommate, whom she'd slept with before she'd met me. She couldn't go one day without fucking me, so

I figured she was getting some on the side while I was gone. I had trust issues.

"You been fucking old boy when I was in jail?" I asked her.

"How can you ask me that?"

But my roommate kept grinning at me, and that drove me crazy.

I wanted to go down to the courthouse and get married right away. She wanted to have a wedding, but she agreed to go to the courthouse. But before we did it, the bartender's mom came up to me and pulled me to the side and said, "You know you're no fucking good for her. Just leave her alone."

"I can't do that," I said. "I love her."

The bartender and her mom didn't want me to marry her because they saw me as a drug dealer and a loser. They'd promised Belinda's parents that they'd look out for her.

The night before we were going to the courthouse to get married, I'm working and get a personal call from the bar.

I go to the bar, and the Amazon bartender says, "That's me. You're taking me home." Belinda is now tending bar there, and I'm taking her girlfriend back to their apartment.

The whole trip there she's trying to talk me out of marrying Belinda. Then she asks me, "What it would take for you to just leave her?"

"Nothing, I love her!"

"Would you like to fuck me?"

I knew it was wrong, but hey, I'm a guy with hormones. So we went inside and her body was spectacular! Everything was on point, and she was muscular. It wasn't great because she had too many muscles.

As soon as we were done, she got her clothes on and said, "Now I got you!"

She calls up Belinda. "I just fucked your boyfriend. He's cheated on you with me!"

I knew I had to get ahead of this. I get in the cab and rush to the bar. Belinda's gone. I find out the next morning, she's at a motel, so I go over there and I told her I was set up. Belinda was so mad at her roommate that she listened to me. And later that day, we did go down to the courthouse and got married.

And for a while there, things were going well, except that I got fired from my taxi job because me and other drivers got caught drag-racing our vehicles.

It wasn't a problem because I quickly found a better job at Lear Siegler in Anaheim in shipping and receiving. I ran the Instapak machine for molding computer packaging.

I had a lot of money so I bought a motorcycle: a 754 Honda, which I'd drive 120 mph on the freeway. I'm going down Beach Boulevard one day, and this milk truck starts to make a left hand turn into my lane and stops. I'm only doing 35 mph at the time, but I couldn't stop, and my bike smashes into his truck. Just before impact I jump up and fly over the milk truck and land in the middle of the road. I was all fucked up with bruises all over my body. They took me to the emergency room, but I'm freaking out because they wanted to take my jean jacket off, which had Thai sticks in one pocket and a quarter-ounce of cocaine in the other pocket. I couldn't take a chance with the cop in the room, who was wanting to take an accident report.

The nurses even wanted to cut my jacket off, but I wouldn't let them, so they made me sign a document that I was refusing medical treatment.

I went home and got healed up and sued the milk truck company. My lawyer got a $25,000 settlement but before the check had arrived, he told me I could use promissory notes to pay my bills and buy some stuff. So I did that, but I had no intention of making good on those notes because I've got a criminal mindset. I stiffed some places for about two grand.

Like a lot of people in L.A., Belinda loved getting celebrity autographs. One day, we saw Robert Blake making a movie in downtown L.A., and my wife wanted his autograph.

So I go up to him and ask him, "Hey, Baretta, can I have your autograph?"

He just turns away.

I tell my wife that he wouldn't give it to us, but she won't take no for an answer.

"You go get that autograph!"

So I go back and repeat: "Hey, Baretta, can I have your autograph?"

"My fucking name isn't Baretta. It's Mr. Blake. Ask me right."

"OK, Mr. Blake, can I have your autograph?"

And I got his autograph.

The marriage didn't last more than a couple years, though.

We had a kid, Matthew, that she got custody of. At least I think it was my kid.

She was always hanging around with guy friends, and I can

read body language well. I'm no fool. They're sitting right next to each other on the couch, and when I come in, they separate.

I didn't like those guys, so we decided to move back to Jonesboro, Arkansas, where her parents lived and where I promised to buy her a house.

On the trip back, she was telling me how her daddy loved Coors beer. So I said, "Let's stop in Colorado and get her dad some beer." We bought 20 cases of Coors beer for her dad, and I took her to the Hill in Boulder and told her all about my escapades there, but the Hill was gone, and there was a police station on the corner.

When we got to Jonesboro, we set the 20 cases of Coors on her dad's front porch. He left it out there for weeks because it was winter time and it stayed cold out there.

We stayed at her parents' house for a bit. I got along well enough with her dad, who would give me advice and take me hunting and fishing with Belinda's brothers. One time I got chased straight up a tree by a razorback. When her brothers arrived, they just laughed at me. One of the brothers had been in the service, so we connected on that level.

But her mother straight up hated me. She was so suspicious of everything I did. "So you spent some time in jail there in California," she'd say.

I finally bought us a cheap-ass house two doors down from her parents. And I got a job at Colson Caster Company, whose slogan was, "They put the world on wheels." There was a strike on, and I crossed the picket line and got a well-paying job as a punch-press operator and inspector. Constantly, the owner would be coming out, screaming at me, and correcting my work, but finally I picked it up.

There was a pretty gal working there, and I started flirting with her, and she'd be flirting with me. Soon enough, I was cheating on Belinda with this gal, and the word got back to her. She wasn't happy about that, but I suspected she was cheating on me, too, because she was always hanging around with her old high school friends, and they were all smoking my dope and drinking my booze.

I call her on it one night, and I tell her to knock it the fuck off.

"How dare you say that to me, you cocksucker. Get out of here."

"This is my fucking house! Go to your parents' house," which was two doors down.

"I'm not leaving."

Unfortunately, her two brothers were there, and they had their baseball bats and beat me bloody on the front lawn. I was barely able to crawl into the car and drive myself to the hospital. I had lacerations on my head and a concussion.

I drove from Jonesboro to Little Rock and parked on the street downtown and slept in my car that night. It was the dead of winter, so I didn't get a good night sleep. I started to look for work the next day, and I got a job selling door to door fire alarms.

They give me this two-hour orientation. Then they give me a briefcase, with the alarm and smoke detector in it. And then out I go to try to sell them.

At first, I couldn't sell these things. About a week later, during one of the worst blizzards in Arkansas history, I'm out on Christmas Eve trying to make sales.

This woman answers the door. I say, "You look just like my mother."

She says, "Bless your heart. Why don't you come on in."

I come in, she gets me something to drink, and a plate of hot food, and I sit by the fire to warm up. She's entertaining some friends that night, and one is a State Representative.

He asked me about the fire alarms I was selling because he'd heard me talk about them at the door.

"Well, I have a whole demonstration that I could show you," I said. "I have a projector right here."

"Oh, movies," she said. "Let's see a movie."

I showed them the whole spiel about how the fire alarm worked. Then I went into the demonstration. I'm holding a lighter next to the fire alarm, and the heat sets the alarm off, which is really loud.

They start laughing. And then they say, "Ok, you can shut it off now."

I say, "You can't shut it off. That's the beauty of it."

I take it outside and I stuff it in a snowbank, and you could still hear it inside, and that makes them laugh again.

She says, "It's definitely loud."

The Senator is impressed: "Here's my card. You should come by my office. We're trying to make it mandatory to have fire alarms in every nursing home in the state."

Next day, I go to the office, and say to the boss, "Look who

I met?" And I show him the State Representative's card. "He wants to put fire alarms all over the place."

We go see the State Representative. He says if my bill goes through, you'll get the contracts for putting fire alarms in every state-run nursing home.

The next week, my boss comes to me and says, "The bill went through, and we got the contract. And that means you're the number one salesman in Arkansas."

The following weekend, he hires a big white limo to take me to Memphis for a sales celebration. They take me to this big banquet, and the keynote speaker is telling everybody what I did, and he introduces me to the crowd as the salesman of the year.

I get up there and I waive at everybody. He hands me a certificate, and then walks me off the stage. I didn't get to say anything.

That night, my boss offered me a hooker and got me drunk. I was still hung over the next morning when the limo came to drive me back to Little Rock.

I checked the mail to see if my commission had arrived yet. I was supposed to be getting $1.2 million for the fire alarm deal, which was bringing the company $12 million.

But the check wasn't there, so I drive down to the office only to find that the doors are locked. I look through the windows and see that the typewriters are gone. The copy machine is gone. Papers are strewn everywhere.

Now I drive over to the boss's house. I knock on the door. No one answers. I peer into the living room, and there was no furniture at all.

Next, I drive over to the vice president's house. He lived in a double-wide trailer. I go up to his door, and it's wide open. There's nothing in there, either.

It was obvious they'd just left town – and left me high and dry.

I was so upset. I went to the State Representative to see if there's a way he could help me get money. He said, "It's out of my hands. They ripped me off, too."

I never got the money. That really hurt. It could have turned my life around there. It was the big break that I needed, but didn't get.

This set me back to my old ways, and I got busted in Little Rock for pimping and pandering and drug possession. A prostitute friend of mine named Rachel gave the bondsman a blowjob to post my bail, so I got out. She also blew my court-appointed attorney because she thought it'd help. I made a deal with court to go into a live-in drug and alcohol program for a year. But after six months, they let me go out to look for work, and I hopped into my car and drove to California.

They put out a warrant for my arrest, charging me with escape and a probation violation.

Back in California, I got busted for selling drugs again.

And guess what? I run into Robert Blake again.

This time, it's in the L.A. County Jail, where he's being held for murdering his wife, a charge that he ended up beating. He's in 4400, the block of cells where they house the celebrities.

My inmate job as a trustee was to deliver food to everyone in 4400 and to place it right outside their doors.

So when I was at Robert Blake's cell door serving him lunch, I wanted to say, "Here you are, Baretta."

After I did my time in the L.A. County Jail, they extradited me to Little Rock. The private company transporting me made a lot of stops on the way back to Arkansas, picking up and dropping off other prisoners. Sometimes we had to stay in a local jail for a couple weeks as we waited for other prisoners to be transported. So it took a while to get back to Little Rock, and when I got there, they put me back in jail for about a month. And then there was a continuance in my case.

When they finally got me in front of a judge, I rose and said, "Your Honor, I'd like to submit a habeas corpus motion to have the charges dismissed because they failed to arraign me within 180 days."

The judge called a recess to "tabulate," he called it. When he came back into court, he said, "You're right. It's been 182 days. Case dismissed!"

———

I almost escaped from prison once. I was back in the City Prison in San Francisco, doing a year and a month. I was locked in the hole again. I remember who was in the cell next to me: Larry Layton, Jim Jones's assistant. He was a squirrelly looking guy, wispy. The only thing he said about Jonestown was that it was a terrible thing that never should have happened. He denied having anything to do with the Kool-Aid. But I could tell he felt guilty about it just by the way he talked about all the little kids dying.

When I got out of the hole, they moved me to an annex of the prison, which was this old stucco-looking monolith on the outskirts of San Francisco. It's like where they send people who aren't a risk or a big troublemaker. It's a reward to go there, and it's easy living and lax security.

I meet this kid, Bob Sargent, and we start playing cards, and we become fast friends. He says he gets out tomorrow. I've been saving up these Thorazine tablets that look like Motrin tablets. My original plan was to save up enough Thorazine so I could sleep for a couple days so the time would go by faster.

But I had a better idea.

We were playing cards the night before Bob gets out. I convince him that if we take five Motrin we'll catch a good buzz with this Pruno, this jailhouse wine, I had on hand. So we're drinking some wine and I give him five pills, which I tell him are Motrin but were, in fact, Thorazine. They actually look alike. So he took 5,000 milligrams of Thorazine, which was a big overdose. He went to sleep. As soon as he was down, I reached across the table and stretched his wrist band out as much as I could, and I pulled it over his hand and then put it on my wrist. Then I dragged him to my cell, and I went over to his cell.

Next morning, they tap on my door, and they say, "You ready to go?"

"Sure am!"

They check the wrist band.

"Right."

They take me downstairs and dress me out and give me his personal belongings. Problem: They give me his clothes, and the clothes don't fit! This kid was 50 pounds lighter and a good six inches shorter than me.

"These are not my fucking clothes," I say.

"Well, it says right here that they're yours," one of the guards says.

"They're not fucking mine!"

"All right." And he goes and finds me something to wear.

He puts me in a van and drives me to the San Diego jail, where Bob was initially processed.

The officer there looks up at me and says, "You're Bob Sargent?"

"Yep."

"And you're supposed to get out today?"

"Well, Bob, tell me something: How come you look so different from the day I arrested you?"

Busted!

So the cop calls the guard over who drove me down.

"You got the wrong guy."

"You son of a bitch," the guard says. "You're not getting out. In fact, you're going to be staying a lot longer."

After six hours in the cell, the door opens up, and they bring in Bob, who was strapped to a two-wheeler.

One of the guards says: "Is this the guy who gave you the pills?

Bob's still barely able to talk, but he nods his head.

The guard says, "You almost killed that kid."

"I didn't do anything," I say, uttering one of my most obvious lies ever.

Bob got released that day. I got another year tacked on.

CHAPTER 11:

FINALLY CAPTURE

During my bank-robbing spree, I never got stopped by an armed guard in any bank, and I never got pulled over by the cops while I was driving away, or while I was moving cross country.

But I did have a few close calls.

Early on, I walked into a Bank of America in San Diego. It said, "Bank of America: Asian Branch."

There was nothing but Asian people everywhere. All the employees were Asian, and all the customers were Asians.

I go up to the teller and say, "High, I just want to cash this check."

She turns it over, sees my note, and hollers at me: "No, you go!"

I didn't know what to do.

I grabbed the note and booked out of there.

Many months later, I was at another bank in California, and the teller was real talkative.

"Hi, how you doing?"

"Fine, you?" I said.

"You not from around here, are you?"

"No, "

Then I'm handing her my check.

"No, I can't. Not if you're not from around here."

She hadn't even turned it over to see my robbery note.

I asked her again and urged her to turn it over and see that it was endorsed.

But she refused.

So all I could think of saying was, "Thank you, thank you," and I headed out.

Then I see the teller in the parking lot with a piece of paper and a pencil. And I thought, "She's getting my license plates."

My third close call was at a bank in Chicago.

As always, I approached the teller and handed her my check. She turned it over, and saw the note, and she wasn't having any of it.

"Unh-uh, honey, I ain't giving you no money. You better get the hell out of here."

Like I was a little kid!

"Well, give me my check back then," I said.

She wouldn't do that.

So I grabbed one end of it, and she held the other, and we tugged at it, and it ripped in half.

She said, "I got half of it now, and you better get the hell on out of here."

And so I did, without further incident.

Eventually, I got complacent and sloppy, and my addictions were getting the better of me.

I was busy robbing banks in the morning and getting high and traveling in the afternoon. There was no hump in the front seat of the Cadillac, so I'd be driving and I'd stretch my legs out after shooting some heroin, and I'd be smoking a blunt and drinking Jack and Coke. Occasionally, I'd nod off while was driving.

Once I drove down into the medium and I had to steer it out going 70. That woke me up!

Another time I nodded off, and the car was fish-tailing when I opened my eyes. So I spun the wheel to the left and to the right, and finally brought the car to a stop in the middle of the highway. Luckily, there were no cars behind me.

I also let up on my carefully planned routine. At the beginning, I made sure, after I robbed the final bank of the day, to drive straight across state lines. But as my spree got longer, I'd often go back to the hotel room and leave later that day. That wasn't smart.

Finally, my luck ran out in Altoona, Iowa.

I was staying at the Playland Motel, right across from Playland Park. That morning, I'm all ready to go. I got my suit on the bed and my briefcase is full of a couple hundred thousand in cash, along with drugs and spoons and needles.

I'm ready to hit a couple banks in town and then leave. But

I'm up so early I decide to go down the road to a little coffee place, which wasn't my routine.

When I get about a mile down the road there's a trooper just sitting in his car by the side of the road. I drive on by. And then right in the middle of the highway, just a little ways ahead, is a big jeep-like vehicle with a cop inside.

"Wow, that's fucking weird," I think to myself.

At the coffee place, there are all sorts of law enforcement vehicles in the parking lot, and I can see that the coffee shop is just packed with them. So I don't go in. I just pull right out of the parking lot and drive back toward my motel. At the exit, there are two state trooper cars off to the side of the road just sitting there.

I take the exit. I grab my garment bags and shove them in the trunk. I go back for my briefcase, and I see these big fat cops at the office. I knew I couldn't check out there!

So I head to the fire exit and up pops this guy with a green jacket.

He wants to get in the fire exit, which is locked from the inside. He asks me if I can let him in. I opened it up for him and he walks by me. On the back of his jacket is "FBI."

I quickly head to my car.

Then I hear, "Hey, hey, hold on a minute."

I turn to the FBI guy and say, "Yeah, what can I do for you?"

"Do you drive a Cadillac?"

"Yes, I do. Why?"

"We're looking for someone driving a Cadillac."

I said, "This red one right here is mine," though my black

one was three cars down.

"Oh, we're looking for a guy driving a black Cadillac."

I thought I was off the hook at that point, but then he asked: "Do you mind opening the trunk?"

"Do you have a warrant?" I asked.

"I don't need a warrant to ask you to open your trunk."

I slipped up here. He was right to say he didn't need a warrant to *ask* me to open the trunk, but he did need a warrant to *force* me to open the trunk. In any event, I thought I might still be able to get out of this jam, so I go to the trunk of the red Cadillac and get out my key and put it in, and I turn it as hard as I possibly can, and the damn thing just wouldn't open.

"You're the guy we've been looking for, aren't you?"

He handcuffed me and took me back to my little hotel room, which by then was swarming, wall to wall, with law enforcement. They had DEA, FBI, ATF, local police, sheriff's deputies, a U.S Marshall, and even a Texas Ranger, who said, with a thick drawl, "I've been hunting you since Texas."

CHAPTER 12:

PRISON FOR 15

They took me to the Polk County jail in Des Moines.

I was prepared. You can tell how much of a junkie I was because here's what I always did on robbery days: I would take two or three grams of heroin and put it in a balloon and shoved it up my ass so I wouldn't be sick in jail with withdrawals if I ever got caught.

So I had a ball of heroin up there when they put me in this holding cell for the first 24 hours. I pulled that ball of heroin out, but I didn't have any syringe or anything.

"I'm a diabetic," I told the guard. "I need insulin and a syringe."

They get the nurse. She checked me out and said, "You're not diabetic."

So I didn't get the syringe.

I asked a guard if he had an ink pen. He wouldn't give it to me.

I started pinching off bits of the heroin ball and let it dissolve in my mouth. I convinced myself it was helping me. I'd take another pinch, and it managed to hold off the throwing up and the diarrhea of withdrawals.

After 24 hours, they came and took me to my cell with with a bunch of other guys. We could look out the windows and see the courthouse, which was on one side, and there was a bank on the other side, though it wasn't a bank that I'd robbed.

Nobody was a diabetic in the cell so there were no syringes. But one guy had a Bic pen, so I tried to make a syringe out of the shaft. I methodically sharpened the tip down on the concrete floor of the cell until I got the perfect point. Then I rubber-banded a balloon to one end of it. I would get a little juice in the balloon, and I could squeeze it through the shaft when I pushed the pen into my arm. But I made a bloody mess. I fucked up my arm bad.

They took me to the hospital, and the doctors had to cauterize the vein shut. Then they sent me back to jail and gave me a mild sedative, which didn't do anything. I went through withdrawals: I was shitting and puking at the same time.

The guys in the cell were nice, and they liked my stories, so they tried to take care of me. They'd give me their soup at dinner or their milk.

When I told them what I was in for, they thought I was the second coming because I did something they'd only seen done in movies.

"Did you use a gun or kill anyone?" they asked.

They wanted me to be John Dillinger.

So I told them that I didn't use a gun, and that I didn't kill anyone. But I told them all how I did it, with the note written on the back of the check.

There was this old guy named William who was very friendly and was totally captivated by my war stories about my criminal escapades. He especially loved my story about how I "hypothetically" robbed banks, and he constantly wanted me to repeat how I did it to the point where I thought he might be a jailhouse snitch who could testify against me in court about what I told him.

I always said that this is "hypothetical" when talking about any crimes that I'd committed, and especially to anybody incarcerated with me, because jailhouse snitches are a real thing. I was approached by an assistant D.A. and an assistant federal prosecutor to become a jailhouse snitch because of my close contact with an inmate they were investigating. They'd offer compensation at several different levels, starting with reducing my sentence all the way to dropping all charges. I wasn't going to be a snitch, but I thought I'd have a little fun with them. I wasn't really a tough guy, but I could play the part. So I'd say, "What else?" And they'd say, "There could be some monetary compensation." And I'd ask them, "Well, how much?" Then they would tell me some piddly amount. And I'd say, "Is that all?" And they'd say, "What do you want?" So I'd lean in and I'd say, "How 'bout an 8-ball of coke and a hooker?" After I said that, they knew there was no way in hell that I would ever rat on another inmate.

Anyway, William would slide up next to me as I was staring out the jailhouse window, and he'd say, "Jerry, how would you rob *that* bank?" So I'd tell him my routine, one more time, and he'd eat it up.

A couple of days before William was due to be released, he was getting extremely excited. Little did I know at the time that he wasn't as excited about getting out as he was in taking a crack at robbing the bank across the street.

The morning he was waiting to get released he cornered me. Once more, he wanted to go over the story of how I did it. So I told him as usual that I would, hypothetically, type on the back of a check a note saying,

"GIVE ME ALL OF THE CASH IN YOUR DRAWER. DON'T ALERT ANYONE OR PRESS ANY ALARM BUTTONS. DON'T GIVE ME THE DYE PACK. I DON'T WANT TO HURT ANYONE!!!!"

Right before he was released, William showed me a piece of paper that he had written his withdrawal request on, grinned, and shook my hand, and walked out of the jail.

Every inmate in there rushed to the jail windows to see what was going to happen next. The windows were five feet tall and four feet across, with bars on the outside, of course. As we looked out, there was William, walking right across the street to the front door of the bank. Then, about 10 minutes later, William popped out the front door and looked lost and confused. First, he turned to the left and started walking, fast, with his head on a swivel. The direction William took led him back to the courthouse, and at this time of the day, the courthouse was crowded with lawyers, cops, criminals, witnesses, judges, and just regular folks that like to sit in on other people's trials because they're curious.

Suddenly, William stops, turns around, and starts running back toward the bank. Talk about your criminal always returning to the scene of the crime! William is so scattered that he runs past the front door of the bank, weaving between customers coming in and out. He takes a hard right at the corner of the building and runs into the parking lot, full of cars and some people. And that was the last we saw of our buddy.

After he disappeared, we all just fell silent, and we didn't know what to say. And then someone said, "Yes!" And we all started cheering and celebrating.

One thing I didn't tell William about and that was, you have to stay low-keyed. You don't want to draw attention to yourself. Unfortunately, William was noticed by many people and by the cameras in the bank. About four or five hours later, William was escorted through the front door of our cell, and as he walked in, he had this enormous grin on his face. Then, right after the jailer locked the door and left, he started jumping up and down, laughing and screaming, "It worked! It fucking worked!"

This is when I realized that William was a few bricks short of a load. If I'd been able to recognize William's mental condition, I wouldn't have told him anything. He just seemed like a nice guy. I didn't actually think he would do it.

He failed to learn to do all the things he needed to do like have a disguise, put superglue on his fingers, and have a getaway car and a plan to leave town right away.

Instead, he ran home, which was two blocks away, and was taken into custody minutes after he arrived. The cops nearly beat him to his own house.

William was still giddy about having pulled off the heist, even for a short time. "It was sort of like the feeling you have right after sex," he told us. "And a helluva rush. And it made my dick hard."

After the fun was over and we were done celebrating for the moment, I started watching TV in the day room with a dozen guys. An ad came on with this young attractive lawyer, telling the world that he wanted to be my attorney, and that he'd represent me with no money up front. In other words, he was the typical ambulance chaser. He specialized in civil matters more so than criminal law, but the print at the bottom of the screen said he'd also handle criminal cases. I thought to myself. "This is the perfect crooked lawyer to defend a crooked person like me." So I wrote down the number and gave his office a call, collect.

I explained my situation to the receptionist, and she talked with the lawyer, who agreed to visit me at the jail.

He comes to the jail and explains he's not really a criminal lawyer but that he used to do it. He wanted to know how I was going to pay him. I told him about the $180,000 I had when the feds arrested me. He said we'll file a motion and try to get it back. He wanted a certain percentage of it. I think 40 percent, or something outrageous like that. I said, they also seized my brand-new Cadillac Eldorado.

His immediate response was: "What color was it?"

"Black."

"I'll take the Cadillac. You sign the Cadillac over to me and I'll represent you."

"I might as well," I said. "I can't drive it in prison." So I signed it over.

The trial was a long, drawn-out process. My lawyer was filing this, that, and the other thing. He tried to get the case dismissed on a technicality. And then he tried to get it dismissed on hearsay. He worked his ass off for me.

But eventually, it came down to witnesses and evidence.

They put all the cops up there, and they presented a lot of documents, and they pointed to a lot of maps, and they revealed all the money I had in my briefcase, so they corroborated everything.

Of course, my lawyer didn't want me to testify at all. He told me all the things that could go wrong. But I insisted. I was so sure I could rebut everything.

I get up there, and the judge asks my attorney if he's ready to question me.

"I have no questions, your honor," he says.

So the prosecutor gets up and says, "Yeah, I have some questions."

He kept me on the stand for 45 minutes. And I'm leaning back, trying to look relaxed. I think I'm being pretty cool, as he's asking me all these questions, and I'm being really vague.

"I don't know," I'd say. "I don't remember."

I feel like I'm doing a good job so I look at my attorney and I smile at him, and he just smiles back at me.

Then the prosecutor asks me a couple questions and says that I need to use more than a couple words when I'm answering him. That's where he tripped me up. I'd given a one-word answer previously that didn't add up to the more elaborate answer I gave to a similar question. And I was hamming it up, telling all sorts of stories on the stand.

Shortly after that, the prosecutor ended his questioning.

"You can step down," the judge said.

I sit down next to my lawyer and say, "See, I told you I'd do a good job."

During closing statements, my attorney stood up and said they haven't proved their case beyond a reasonable doubt, and he tossed in a bunch of legal jargon.

Then the prosecutor gets up and he says: "I want to thank Mr. Heckathorn for being such a colorful individual on the witness stand."

And he stepped down.

I lean over to my attorney, "See, he liked what I said."

My attorney leaned back to me and said, "He just called you a fucking liar."

So, that was that.

I was sentenced to 18 months at Anamosa State Prison in Iowa. It was called the Castle, and it was really an evil place.

I spent a considerable amount of time in the hole, which

was on the top floor of the prison. In Iowa, in the summertime, it's very, very hot. The sun beating down on those top cells made it insufferable. You'd just sweat profusely. You had to stand in the toilet and flush it to cool down. And you'd take the cold toilet water and pour it over your heads. It was the only thing you could do.

It was a horrible, horrible place.

I knew I was in for a long haul even after the Castle because there were holds on me from a dozen different states waiting to arrest me upon release. I was going to be charged in one state after another.

The next place they took me to was Arizona. The feds picked me and five other inmates up in a diesel van and drove us west. Before we got to the county jail, they stopped off at a plywood makeshift jail right in the middle of nowhere right outside of Midland-Odessa, Texas. All you saw was rocks and dirt.

The plywood was only three-quarters of an inch think, so four of the inmates just kicked it out and escaped. I didn't go with them because there was a chance I could get out in six months if they honored my time served in Iowa. Plus, there was nowhere to run in the desert.

The next morning, the feds show up and they throw me and the other guy who stayed behind on the ground and hand-cuffed us.

"Why are you doing this to us?" I asked. "We're the ones that didn't escape."

They caught the other four guys in no time at all.

They dropped me off at the federal prison in Safford. They

had one unit where they brought down these high-profile inmates from Alaska. They were Innuits, and they'd never go outside because it was so hot. I thought that was cruel and unusual, too, to put them there.

A couple days later I was vanned to the county jail in Phoenix, where they arraigned me. They gave me a public defender, and he was a good one.

He made a deal with the prosecutors to agree to credit me with time served in Iowa. So when I got 24 months in Arizona, I only had to do six months. He told me to try to get time served every place I'd be sent after that.

Next stop, the Northwest New Mexico Correctional Center. There were a lot of sick people there: Sexual deviants, and mentally challenged people who didn't belong in jail. And the mentally ill guys were treated like shit. Verbally abused, if not physically abused. Punished for being mentally handicapped. It was just wrong.

Every federal prison was exactly the same. The same layout. The same blue paint. After a while, it was hard to remember where I was.

My favorite place was the MCC in Chicago, the Metropolitan Correctional Center, downtown. I just met so many interesting people in there. I'm talking about cartel members, high-priority gang leaders, major drug dealers. Some of them didn't even speak English, but they were nice. I made some friends in there -- some contacts I thought I 'd use when I got out.

From there, I was extradited to Wisconsin. This was the

only state that would not give me credit for time served in other states. I'd already served twelve and a half years, and Wisconsin wouldn't run the time I owed them concurrent with the time I'd served already. So they sentenced me to two and a half years in state prison, and eight years' probation.

I went to intake at the Dodge Correctional Facility, and then I was taken to Waupun. The place was a nightmare.

There were so many gangs in there, it was ridiculous. There were Mexican gangs, and the Southern United La Raza. The Latin Kings were there, too. So were the Black gangs, mainly splinter groups from the Bloods and the Crips. Of course, there were white gangs: the Aryan Brotherhood, skinheads, and neo-Nazis. Each of these gangs had their own language and codes.

Many of the inmates were downright scary, especially the sexual predators and the other sociopaths. And the guards were sadistic: They enjoyed watching the inmates go at each other, and when they'd come into the hole to punish an inmate, it wasn't a fair fight. They'd have these padded shields and they'd be swinging their billy clubs and they'd back the inmate up against the cell wall and beat the living shit out of him and then haul him off to the hole.

In the hole, the yelling between the shot-callers of the Aryan Brotherhood guys and the Black gang members was constant, and the noise in the place was insane. Several guys would be barking like dogs. Another group sounded like cats. A couple of guys would be yelling out obscenities at no one in particular. That would prompt another inmate to yell, "Shut up! Shut up!"

Meanwhile, a group of gangbangers would be rapping: "If your bitch woulda been right in da head, she wouldn't be layin' in the cold morgue dead."

One way I survived in Waupun was by selling good hamburgers to the other inmates. I got a job in the kitchen, and I became friends with one of the cooks there. After our shifts were over, we'd stay back and he'd make these giant hamburgers with eggs, cheese, bacon, just the works. He'd wrap them up and we'd smuggle them out to sell down the main line.

He got busted for making wine in the kitchen. So that was the end of my catering business, but it had made me popular for a while.

Another way I survived was by being a jail-house lawyer. Other inmates would see me in the prison library researching appeals for my own case, and they'd ask me to draft appeals for theirs. I never won one for them, but at least I gave them hope.

"This might just work," I'd tell them. And when it didn't, I'd say, "Don't worry. I'll file another appeal for you this afternoon. Put some more money on my books."

They paid me $150-$300 a month. It wasn't much, considering the fact that I was in the library typing eight hours a day and filing all this paperwork shit.

But it was a good deal all around. They got a glimmer of hope, which you need in the joint, and I got canteen money.

Other inmates started looking at me as a problem solver. "What do I do about this, or what do I do about that?"

For instance, I drafted a letter for inmates who hadn't heard from their wives or girlfriends for a while. It would start out:

"Baby, baby, baby, why are you so mean? It's been a good two weeks now, and not one letter have I seen. I feel like something's happened, but I hope you've met no harm. But since I haven't got a letter, I assume you broke your fucking arm. So why don't you do us both a favor and start to feel better. And get off your ass and write me a mother-fucking letter. Love, me. Send money, bitch!"

Almost every inmate got a response. They weren't all favorable, but some of them actually were.

They don't allow smoking in Waupun. But you can smuggle anything into the prison. So this dude had tobacco and some papers and he was asking around for some matches.

"You don't need no matches," I told him. "Just give me a pencil, a paper clip, and a piece of toilet paper."

I explained this trick I'd picked up along the way. You take the toilet paper, hold it to the pencil, bend the paper clip around till you have two prongs sticking out, and you stick those prongs into a socket. It's called "popping a socket." It ignites the toilet paper, you bend down, and you light the cigarette.

Usually, it works. But it didn't this time.

I popped the socket, and the toilet paper caught on fire all right, but so did most of the insulated wire inside the concrete walls. I'd shorted out the electrical system. The day room filled with toxic smoke. We couldn't barely breathe. We banged on the metal door to get the guard's attention. We were snitching on ourselves essentially. The guards come, and they handcuff us and take us to the hole.

Here's how they take you to the hole: They shackle your legs, handcuff your hands behind your back, and they take another pair of shackles and connect one to your handcuffs and one to your leg shackles. Then a couple guards pick up that chain and carry you like a suitcase to the hole. They toss your ass into the cell, and there you sit.

I got charged for burning up that room. They gave me a major write up and a disciplinary hearing and locked me in the hole for six months. But I actually spent 18 months in there because I'm a fuck-up, and I would keep getting time added on for disrespecting the guards or the nurse.

One way I survived all this time in the hole was through yoga and meditation. I did a lot of yoga in Waupun.

But my hygiene wasn't very good. In fact, it was so bad that my armpit hairs turned to rubber because I wasn't able to shower for weeks on end and I had a vitamin deficiency. Eventually the nurse told me that I needed to keep myself cleaner.

"Clean yourself in your sink if you can't get to the shower," she said.

After I got out of the hole at Waupun, I finished up my time at Dodge Correctional and Fox Lake Correctional, which were much better places.

As my release date approached, I was getting excited. To get released, you got to get signatures from just about everyone in authority that you've been interacting with there. There's a whole checklist of people who have to sign off. So I had the work boss sign my card, and the teacher sign my card. I got all the paperwork done.

The day before my release, they called me up to the property room and I'm wondering why they're calling me up because I don't have any property. The sergeant pushes this plastic bag to me, and it's got a Rolex Presidential in it. "I bet you're glad to get this back," he said.

I said, "I certainly am!"

It wasn't mine, of course, but yeah, I was sure glad to have it.

On the day of your release, you have to have your own release clothes, and if you don't have your own clothes, you're released in your prison garb. I didn't have a chance to go shopping or have anyone outside send me new clothes, so I was waiting to get out in my prison clothes.

They called me up to the gate. I showed them my green prison ID card.

The guard at the gate said, "OK, head on out." And he added, with a joke he must have used a thousand times: "I'll see you next week."

At first when you get out, you feel great because you're free. But it's short-lived. Because now you have all these immediate problems: Where am I going to live? What am I going to do for work? And I'm going to have to report to my parole officer every week.

There's more pressure on you after you get out than there is when you're inside. No one's taking care of you anymore. You have to do everything yourself now.

Getting out is scary!

CHAPTER 13:

RETIRING IN MADISON

From the gate at Fox Lake Correctional, they put me in a van and drove me to the big building on East Washington Avenue in Madison and put me in a holding cell at the Department of Corrections headquarters for an hour or so. And then they drove me to a cheap hotel on the west side of Madison right off the Beltline and gave me a two-week voucher for it. The hotel was for ex-convicts who were in the process of reentry. When he drops me off, the van driver hands me a piece of paper with the hotel rules on it. And he emphasizes one of them: "If someone knocks on your door, don't answer it. They're only going to bring you trouble, or get you into drugs or whoring."

So I go in my room and the first couple of days, I get knocks on the door, and I don't even bother with them. On the third day, I answered the knock.

"What do you want?" I asked.

"Hey, you want to get high?" one of the guys said.

I declined.

A day later, I move out of the hotel, and I stay at the Grace Episcopal Church on the corner of West Washington Avenue and the Square for a few days.

I go out every day and I look for work, and finally I got a job with Badger Cab. The manager took pity on me after I told him my life story.

"I'm going to give you a chance," he said.

I had to go through a lot of bullshit to get a permit to drive the cab. I had to go downtown and talk to a sergeant.

"Why the fuck should I give you a permit so you could go sell drugs?"

"I'm done doing that," I said.

But he kept at me, screaming in my face and warning me, in no uncertain terms, not to fuck up again. I had to piss in a cup to prove I wasn't doing drugs. And I had to give him my fingerprints and get a mugshot. He finally gave me my cab driver's license. And as I was leaving, he said, "I do that with anybody who's got a record."

As soon as I got back to Badger Cab, the other drivers had smiles on their faces. "How did you like the Sarge?" one of them said, and they all started to laugh. From then on, whenever another ex-con would join Badger Cab and have to go downtown to get his license, I'd ask him, "How did you like the Sarge?"

Turns out I didn't take the Sarge's advice.

Another job I had was working at the Crystal Corner bar. I was living in the apartment above the bar and would take the stage down after the music acts were done, or put the stage up before they arrived, and I'd clean up.

But I also sold drugs at the Crystal. I got a hold of this old guy I'd met at the MCC in Chicago. Him and his son had a house here in Madison across from Oscar Mayer. It was a dope house. They'd have duffel bags full of kilos they'd stash there.

So I gave him a call.

"Where you at?" I asked.

"We're up in Madison right now."

"I'm here, too.

"Why don't you come over to the house?"

I get there, and we start drinking, and then we talk business. He'd give me a bunch of kilos on commission. So we had a deal.

I sold a few kilos to the biker gang here in town, and the rest I'd sell in quarter pound or ounces to everybody else. Customers would be lining up at the Crystal. We'd go down the stairs and do the deals.

All the bartenders knew I was selling weed. When I'd come up, they'd say: "We know what's going on, you know."

Then one winter morning, bright and early, the cops busted me.

I hear a whole bunch of people coming up the stairs. I'm still in bed, and I got a feeling about what's coming, and I just sit on the edge of the bed and wait.

There's a knock on the door, and a woman yells: "Parole officer! Open the door!"

The man yells, "Police, open the door!"

So I open the door. I'd thought about chucking the weed out the back window but I didn't have time.

The woman was my parole agent, and she asked, "Gerald, do you have any weapons in here?"

"No," I said.

"Do you have any drugs?"

"Yep, there some keys in the back bedroom."

Back to jail I went.

I made a deal with the district attorney's office for six months on Huber: I could work in the community during the days, but I had to go sleep in the county jail at night.

Then I got a job Northern Plating. I told one of the brothers who owned the business that I was on Huber and I was looking for a chance to turn my life around.

"OK, I'll give you that chance," he said.

I worked there for a while. I had a 401(k) there and everything. But I was drinking every day, and I eventually got fired for drinking and for fighting with one of my fellow employees who didn't want to do his share of the work.

So I went back to driving cab.

By this time, I'd given up the drug dealing and was just trying to stay alive.

I had Hep-C for many years, and it was finally diagnosed here in Madison after I got Medicare.

"We don't have anything for you," the doctor told me on the first visit. "There's no cure for it. You've got about six months to live."

In less than one year, I had dropped 120 pounds. I was wasting away.

Every month, I'd go back to the doctor. He'd see how fast I was depreciating.

Then, on one visit, he said: "I might have some good news for you. There's a drug about to be approved by the FDA. It's called Harvoni."

Two or three weeks later, he gave me my Harvoni.

"Take this for 60 days."

When I returned after those two months, he said, "Take it for another 30 days."

You know what? After the 90 days, I was cured. There was no trace of Hep-C in my body. My liver has regenerated itself.

So I was lucky that time.

I was also lucky to get a bank account in the Madison area. Problem was I'd robbed lots of banks here.

There was the M&I bank near Players Bar.

There was the Associated Bank, near East Towne mall.

There was a Home Savings branch, but not the one downtown. I never robbed the downtown banks.

There was US Bank off of Cottage Grove Road by Sprecher Road and the Metro Market, about a mile from where I'm writing this memoir at the Pinney Library on the East Side of Madison.

And there was my favorite, Park Bank, on High Crossing Boulevard near Sun Prairie.

I'll tell you why it's my favorite.

When I got out and moved to Madison, I wanted to open

up a checking account and get a debit card. I thought if I went to the banks that I robbed and apologized for what I'd done and offered to help make their banks safer by identifying their vulnerabilities, they might let me open an account and get a debit card.

I struck out at the first two banks, but the manager at Park Bank was more agreeable. Oh, don't get me wrong. He didn't take me up on my offer to help him safeguard his place.

"I really shouldn't be walking around showing a guy who stole money from my bank where everything is," he said.

He thought I might have been casing the joint.

We both laughed about it.

"I can see your point," I said.

But he heard my sob story.

"I'm sorry for robbing your bank, but I paid for my crimes, and I just need somebody to help me open an account," I told him.

To my surprise, he said, "OK, I'll give you a bank account and a debit card."

The others wouldn't even give me a fucking bank account. I couldn't even give them money!

That's why I'm still at Park Bank to this day.

CHAPTER 14:

REFLECTIONS
AND REMORSE

I'm 73 years old now, and I've got emphysema, but I'm doing
OK. I'm still living in Madison, Wisconsin. I'm playing poker
regularly. I smoke a little weed. But that's pretty much it.

I've been off heroin for 20 years now. I got over it by being
in prison for so long. There's a very sporadic supply of it in
prison. Everywhere I went, I tried to get a hold of some. But
we'd maybe only get enough to get a dozen guys addicted, and
then we couldn't get any more for a month, and the guys would
get sick, and they'd be having withdrawals.

Eventually, as B.B. King would say, the thrill was gone. All
the effort to get the shit in, and all the worry about who you can
trust, got to be more than overwhelming, so I just had to stop.

I missed it for a long time, and I think about it now and again. It was a big part of my life. But I also watch the news, and I know that fentanyl has ruined heroin. You're lucky if you can even find pure heroin anymore.

I also quit drinking, by and large. I used to have a beer for breakfast and then I'd drink beer all day until nighttime, when I'd start with the Jack and Coke. But now I only have a Jack and Coke if I'm at the final table of some poker tournament.

Quitting the heroin and booze was hard. But quitting the guilt's been even harder.

Looking back on what I did during my life, I'll often just say to myself, "I'm a terrible person."

I feel guilty about all the people I affected.

I feel guilty about how I used and abused my family, especially my pops, who would do anything for me. Me and him were really close, and I treated him like shit.

I feel guilty because I wasn't able to go to his funeral, or to my mom's. I was in prison both times, and the wardens wouldn't let me out.

I feel guilty about all the tellers I robbed, and how that must have made them feel. I hope I didn't ruin their lives, but I'm sure I put a hiccup in their lives or disrupted their lives even worse.

I feel guilty about that old man that I knocked down when he was chasing my buddy out of the bank. I found out later that the old guy had a heart attack afterwards and barely survived.

I feel guilty about the kid in my cell with me that I almost killed with Thorazine when I tried switching identities with him.

I even feel guilty about some of the drug deals, especially

when I'd get people so hooked that their lives went to hell.

I was a con man. I was always hustling, trying to get an edge, working the angles. Now I look back at all the people I screwed over. There's cause and effect. And I've caused a lot of bad effect.

I'm just guilt-ridden about it all.

I ask God every day to lift that guilt. But I still feel guilty. Little things come up that trigger me, and this whole book has been one big trigger.

Every day I wake up with the Lord's Prayer. I always pray, and I ask for forgiveness, and for God to release the guilt for me. But it's still there.

The funny thing is they used to ask me at sentencing, "Do you wish to express any remorse?"

And my attorney would say, "Show some remorse."

It was so hard for me. I didn't know what the word meant back then.

I'd say I was sorry, but I didn't mean it.

Judges would tell me, "You're just sorry that you got caught."

Which was true. I never had remorse. But now I have it.

After the fog of drugs and alcohol lift and you get back to being more normal, you start to realize all these things that you've done. The more you think about it, the harder it gets.

But I'm enjoying my family these days. My sisters and me are still tight. I've gone out to California and visited them a couple times, and they might come out here to visit me soon.

Two years ago, one of my sisters did that 23andMe thing with our DNA. And we found out we had a half-brother we never knew existed, who was living in Mexico. I have another half-brother who's living on some tropical island who I hadn't seen in 30 years. So my sister set up a Zoom call with all of us, and that was a great time!

Now we're talking about having a family reunion in person, which I'd really like to do.

For kicks and the old adrenaline rush, I still play Texas Holdem, which I've been doing for decades now. I like the camaraderie. I'm good at reading people, as you might imagine. And I'm patient, so that helps. I do OK: I won a couple tournaments at the Ho Chunk Casino in Wisconsin Dells, and I won $52,000 in a Mid-States Poker Tournament.

Got to admit: It's still fun to make money in a non-traditional way.

Thanks for staying with me to the end of my story. I hated writing it, but I hope you loved reading it.